The TEA Book

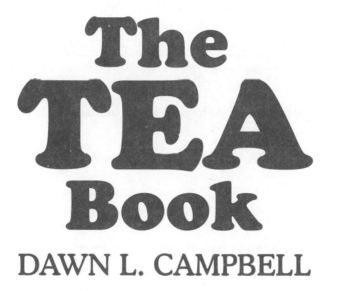

The TEA Book

DAWN L. CAMPBELL

PELICAN PUBLISHING COMPANY
Gretna 1995

*The word "Pelican" and the depiction of a pelican are trademarks
of Pelican Publishing Company, Inc.,
and are registered in the U.S. Patent and Trademark Office.*

Library of Congress Cataloging-in-Publication Data

Campbell, Dawn.
    The tea book / Dawn L. Campbell.
       p. cm.
    Includes index.
    ISBN 1-56554-074-3
    1. Tea. 2. Tea—History. 3. Cookery (Tea) I. Title.
TX817.T3C26 1995
641.3'372—dc20   94-31638
                                                        CIP

Illustrations by Ian Finlayson

Manufactured in the United States of America

Published by Pelican Publishing Company, Inc.
1101 Monroe Street, Gretna, Louisiana 70053

To my grandmother Grace Elizabeth Campbell,
who loved her teatimes

"Take some more tea," the March Hare said to Alice, very earnestly.

"I've had nothing yet," replied Alice in an offended tone, "so I can't take more."

"You mean, you can't take *less,*" said the Hatter: "It's very easy to take *more* than nothing."

—Lewis Carroll, *Alice in Wonderland*

Contents

Preface

Tea is a simple drink and since its introduction over four millennia ago, it has warmed the insides of billions of Earth's inhabitants. Today over 2.5 million tons of tea are cultivated annually in over 30 countries throughout the world. The United Kingdom alone imports over 352 million pounds of tea a year, with the British public sipping over 180 million "cuppas" a day.

The Tea Book is the first book of its kind to focus solely on tea drink recipes and tea-drinking customs from various cultures around the world, demonstrating tea's long and varied sipping history.

As tea migrated around the world, each new tea-drinking region embraced it, introducing to the tea drink its own unique blend of flavoring ingredients and cultural habits. As a result, the customs for the making and the enjoying of tea are as varied and remarkable as the cultures from which they have come.

It is the author's hope that the recipes in this book will open up a wealth of cultural tea-drinking experiences for tea lovers everywhere. I encourage each and every one of you to experiment with these recipes as you journey to the tea tables around the world.

A tea shrub.

Abbreviations

STANDARD			METRIC		
tsp.	=	teaspoon	ml.	=	milliter
tbsp.	=	tablespoon	l.	=	liter
oz.	=	ounce	g.	=	gram
qt.	=	quart	kg.	=	kilogram
lb.	=	pound	mg.	=	milligram

Standard-Metric Approximations

⅛ teaspoon	=	.6 milliliter		
¼ teaspoon	=	1.2 milliliters		
½ teaspoon	=	2.5 milliliters		
1 teaspoon	=	5 milliliters		
1 tablespoon	=	15 milliliters		
4 tablespoons	=	¼ cup	=	60 milliliters
8 tablespoons	=	½ cup	=	118 milliliters
16 tablespoons	=	1 cup	=	236 milliliters
2 cups	=	473 milliliters		
2½ cups	=	563 milliliters		
4 cups	=	946 milliliters		
1 quart	=	4 cups	=	.94 liter

Solid Measurements

½ ounce	=	15 grams		
1 ounce	=	25 grams		
4 ounces	=	110 grams		
16 ounces	=	1 pound	=	454 grams
1 standard measure	=	1 teaspoon		
1 jigger	=	1½ ounces		

1 pound tea yields 200 cups of tea

3,200 first-flush flowers and leaves yield 1 pound of tea

*According to Western research, 6 ounces is the amount of liquid required to extract the maximum amount of tea essence from 1 teaspoon of loose tea in a 5-minute period before the tea becomes bitter.

Acknowledgments

The author would like to thank her friends who have contributed information and many tea-chatting hours towards the development of this book.

My heart goes out to David Burton for not drowning in his teacup while spending endless hours typing and retyping this manuscript. I thank him and Barbara Ladouceur and Veronica Kempkes, who each edited one of the many drafts of this book. Veronica, your keen eye and scrutiny were most appreciated.

Many thanks to Ian Finlayson for his creative and artistic illustrations.

I would also like to express my appreciation to Wah Yuen, Bella Kopan, Tamiko Kishimoto, Le Huang Tan, and Sharon Weston, all of Victoria, for allowing me to photograph their "tea things" for illustrative purposes.

Special "cups o' cheer" to my friends from around the globe who have shared with me their knowledge of recipes and tea-drinking customs from various countries. Beside each person's name is listed the country/ies on which he or she contributed information. Thanks to Nargis (Afghanistan, Libya), Karl (Austria), Loocho (Bolivia, Chile), my mom, Ruth (Brazil), Ruth (Chile), Cynthia (China), Magdalena (The Czech Republic, Slovakia), Elias (Ethiopia), Kamal (India), Pauline (Ireland), Kazuko and Naoko (Japan), Angelina (Lebanon, Syria), Sylvie (Nepal), Nina and Martin (The Netherlands), Nunsy (Norway), Yarka (Poland), Bruce (Portugal), Jessica (Taiwan), Toochi (Uganda), and Van, Sharon, and Tan (Vietnam).

Arigoto to Tamiko Kishimoto for reviewing my work on *Ochaji,* the Japanese Tea Ceremony. Having been a member of the *Omete Senke* School of Tea for many years, Tamiko is exceptionally knowledgeable in the intricacies of this ceremony.

Thanks also to Cynthia for her Mandarin translations, Kamal for her translations in Hindi and Moroccan, Peg for her consultations in Russian, and Eloise for reviewing my French translations.

The following personnel from the embassies to Canada were all very gracious and helpful in responding to my enquiries on tea drinking. I gratefully acknowledge the High Commission of the Republic of Kenya (Wachira Nyaga), the Sri Lanka High Commission (Pushpa Ailapperuma), the High Commission of the United Republic of Tanzania (Rose Mapka), the Embassy of the Republic of Tunisia (Sehim Seltene), and the Embassy of the Republic of Zaire (Dali Peng).

I tip my cup to the staff in the Interlibrary Loan Department of the Greater Victoria Public Library for taking my endless supply of interlibrary loan notices and for their dedication to tracking down books for me, both nationally and internationally.

My gratitude to Lyons Tetley Limited, R. Twining & Co. Ltd., and The Stash Tea Company for responding so quickly to my enquiries and for granting me permission to quote from their literature.

And finally, but certainly not least of all, I would like to thank my editor at Pelican Publishing Company, Nina Kooij, for the expertise she brought to *The Tea Book* and its earlier companion volume, *The Coffee Book*.

The TEA Book

The Story of Tea

The Legends of Its Origins

No one really knows how "tea" first came into being. However, throughout its long history, tea has had many divine myths attributed to its origins.

The most popular myth depicting tea's early discovery is associated with one of China's first emperors, Shen nung, who reigned from 2737 to 2697 B.C. and was considered by the Chinese to be the "Son of Heaven." Shen nung chanced upon tea while he was boiling water for purification. As fate would have it, a leaf from a nearby tree fluttered into the pot of boiling water. Within minutes, the aroma rising from the pot tempted Shen nung to taste the decoction. He became so enamored of tea that he ordered his loyal subjects to begin the planting of it. With the growing of tea came the need for the development of agricultural techniques and, more significantly, the change in mankind's behavior from gathering to cultivating food.

Another wondrous Chinese legend has it that tea originated in India, where it grew wild in the hills of Assam. During the Han Dynasty (A.D. 25-221), the Chinese sent a scholar named Gan Lu to India to study Buddhism. When he returned to China, Gan Lu brought back with him his newfound religious beliefs in Buddhism and some Assam tea seeds. With the planting of these seeds came the cultivation of tea in China.

Indian Buddhists have yet another legend about the discovery of tea. According to their version, Buddha travelled to China to take up meditation for a planned nine years. During his fifth year of meditating, the inevitable happened. Buddha suffered the effects of fatigue and found it all but impossible to meditate. As he nodded off to sleep, unknowingly he grabbed some twigs from a nearby tree and chewed them. Within an instant, he was miraculously restored to an alert and contemplative state. The aid to his recovery was none other than the divine tea plant.

Legends continued, and three thousand years after the time of Shen nung, tea finally made its way with travelling Chinese monks to the developing nation of Japan. Tea, as in China, became so influential in Japan's culture that the Japanese developed their own myth of its discovery. Bodhidharma (Dharma), the Japanese believe, was meditating, and became drowsy. So as not to fall asleep, he cut off his eyelids and threw them to the ground. The eyelids miraculously sprouted and grew into tea plants.

17

The Great Tea Debate

By the 1600s, the English had finally heard about *t'e* from authors who wrote about their travels in the Far East. In 1600, Queen Elizabeth I established the British East India Company because she wanted to find the much talked about *t'e* for her people. However, as history would have it, bringing the tea to England would take yet another fifty years. The English repeatedly tried to establish trade with China, but were continually rejected because the mannerisms of the English traders were perceived by the Chinese as being barbaric. And, comparatively speaking, they were. China, at that time in history, was the most advanced civilization in the world.

Meanwhile, by 1610, the seafaring Dutch traders successfully brought Chinese tea to the European continent from Macao, a Portuguese trading outpost of the Cathay Empire. The Dutch traders also brought green tea to the continent from Japan. As tea poured into the West, it became the focus of much heated debate.

The Continentals, it would seem, would not accord the same divine and medicinal attributes to tea as did the peoples of the East. The first prominent European to question publicly the traditional Chinese belief that tea was a medicinal elixir was a German physician named Simon Paulli. Paulli claimed that "tee is nothing more than a common myrtle, which will hasten the death of those who drink it" (*Commentarius de Abusu Tabaci et Herbae Thee,* by Simon Paulli, Rostock, Germany, 1635).

Vigorously opposing Paulli's view was a Dutch physician named Nikolas Dirx. He claimed that "those who use it [tea] are for that reason alone exempt from all maladies and reach an extreme old age" (*Observationes Medicae,* Amsterdam, 1641).

The debate boiled on for decades, with each side calling the other's kettle black. Eventually the controversy made way for the most well known (and perhaps the most influential!) of Europe's tea-drinking advocates to state his views. A Dutchman, Dr. Cornelius Brontekoë (nicknamed "Dr. Good Tea"), in his *Diatribe de Febribus* (Amsterdam, 1683) prescribed drinking forty to fifty cups of tea a day to reduce high fever—and if that was not enough, he thought even a hundred cups a day would not be too much. Later it was discovered that the renowned Dr. Brontekoë (whose real name, by the way, was Cornelius Decker) just may have been richly rewarded by merchants of the Dutch East India Company for his publicly proclaimed tea prescriptions. It should be noted, however, that Cornelius Decker really was a doctor.

Tea finally did reach England, where in 1658 it was first served and sold publicly at Thomas Garway's well-known coffeehouse in London's Exchange Alley. In 1660, Garway spouted his views with a broadside that he entitled "An Exact Description of the Growth, Quality and Vertues of the Leaf TEA." The famous broadside, now housed in the Museum of London, reads as follows:

The Drink is proclaimed to be most wholesome, preserving in perfect health until extreme Old Age.

The particular virtues are these:

It maketh the Body active and lusty.

It helpeth the Head-ach, giddiness and heaviness thereof.

It removeth the Obstructions of the Spleen.

It is very good against the Stone and Gravel, cleansing the Kidneys and Uriters being drunk with Virgin's Honey instead of sugar.

It taketh away the difficulty of breathing, opening Obstructions.

It is good against Lipitude, Distillations, and cleareth the sight.

It removeth Lassitude, and cleareth and purifieth adult Humors and a hot Liver.

It is good against Crudities, strengthening the weakness of the Ventricle or Stomack, causing good Appetite and Digestion, and particularly for Men of corpulent Body and such as are the great eaters of Flesh.

It vanquisheth heavy Dreams, easeth the Brain, and strengtheneth the Memory.

It overcometh superfluous Sleep, and prevents Sleepiness in general, a draught of the Infusion being taken, so that without trouble whole nights might be spent in study without hurt to the Body, in that it moderately heateth and bindeth the mouth of the stomach.

It prevents and cures Agues, Surfets and Feavers, by infusing a fit quantity of the Leaf, thereby provoking a most gentle Vomit and breathing of the Pores, and hath been given with wonderful success.

It (being prepared and drank with Milk and Water) strengtheneth the inward parts, and prevents consumption, and powerfully assuageth the pains of the Bowels, or griping of the Guts or Looseness.

It is good for Colds, Dropsies and Scurveys, if properly infused purging the Blood of Sweat and Urine, and expelleth Infection.

It driveth away all pains in the Collick proceeding from Wind, and purgeth safely the Gall.

And that the Vertues and excellencies of this Leaf and Drink are many and great is evident and manifest by the high esteem and use of it (especially of late years) among the Physitians and knowing men in France, Italy, Holland and other parts of Christendom. . . .

Garway's public tribute to tea strongly hinted at the popularity this new drink would one day have the world over. As the English trod home from Garway's Coffee House, little did they know that these first sips would soon bring them, too, under tea's divine spell. As the cups of this nation filled with the new brew, tea drinking would spread so rapidly among the English that soon the word "tea" itself would become synonymous with the English everywhere.

The Greatest Tea Clipper Race in history (1866).

The History and Migration of Tea

When we steep our tea leaves we are continuing in a tradition that is several thousand years old. From its origins in the Far East, where it was praised as a medicinal, to its migration to the West, where it was appreciated as a drink of comfort and pleasure, tea has become the national drink of many countries. With the quest to find and cultivate more quantities of it, to fill the need of increasing numbers of tea lovers, tea has had nothing less than a captivating history in the part it has played in the social, economic, and political affairs of the world. The following chronology highlights some of tea's most memorable events along its journey to becoming one of the world's most popular drinks.

The Origin of Tea

There are varying legends as to whether tea originated in India or in China. Some scholars believe it originated in the jungles of the Assam province of India. Others claim it had its earliest beginnings in the Bohea Mountains of the Fukien province of China. Still others suggest that it was native to the Yangtze Valley in the Szechuan province of China.

Tea in China

2737 B.C.   According to a popular legend, one of China's first emperors, Shen nung, happened upon the tea drink when a leaf from a nearby tea plant accidentally fell into a pot of water that he was boiling for purification. The tempting aroma prompted him to taste the brew. Hereby "the world's first cup of tea" was drunk.

1200 B.C.   Early documentation indicates tea was served to King Wen, founder of the Zhou Dynasty.

A.D. 350   Tea is growing along the Yangtze River in Szechuan province.

21

780   "The Tea Classic," *Ch'a Ching,* is written by Lu Yu, a Chinese orphan turned Buddhist scholar. The *Ch'a Ching,* written in three volumes, explains how tea is made and how it should be drunk.

Tribute Tea was produced during this period. The name of this famous tea originated when a courier of the Chinese court tasted the tea from Yang-Hsien. He brought some of the tea to the emperor. Soon all of the imperial family, the palace members, and the aristocracy were drinking copious amounts of tea. As the orders for more and more quantities of tea poured in, tea cultivation (a tribute to the imperial family) spread to many provinces. In order to transport it, Tribute Tea was fired, powdered, and pressed into a paste. The paste was then molded into a cake.

1107   Emperor Hui Tsung (1082-1135) writes a treatise on tea called *Ta Kuan Ch'a Lun.* It is unusual for an emperor, living in isolation from the mass of his subjects, to be able to write so accurately about the many aspects of tea.

Tea in India

Another legend of the Far East claims tea originated in India. Gan Lu, a Chinese scholar who lived during the Later Han Dynasty (A.D. 25-221), went to India to study Buddhism. When he returned to China, he brought back with him his newfound beliefs in Buddhism and tea.

Tea in Japan

A.D. 727   Tea is presented to Emperor Shomu as an official gift from the Chinese T'ang Court. Tea's spread into Japan, however, will be disrupted as the country enters into civil wars. It will be cut off from China for over four hundred years.

794   Tea seeds are planted in the Imperial Gardens in Heian (Kyoto).

900   Tea is brought to Japan by monks who had visited China to study Buddhism.

1191   After centuries of civil strife in Japan, trade with China is renewed. Ch'an Buddhists have begun a ritual of sharing tea that will later influence the development of the Japanese Tea Ceremony.

A Japanese Buddhist monk named Eisai goes to China and returns with tea seeds. These are planted and tea begins its cultivation in Japan. Eisai (1141-1215) also writes the first Japanese tea book.

1400s   Tea drinking finally becomes popular among the masses in Japan.

1477   Shogun Ashikaga-Yoshimasa (1435-90) employs a Buddhist priest named Murata Shuko (1422-1502) to serve tea in ceremonial fashion at his palace near Kyoto. At the same time, Yoshimasa creates the first tearoom to add to his palace. Shuko creates rules of etiquette for what is called *chanoyu* or "hot-water tea."

1584   Sen-no Rikyu (1522-91) is believed to have developed the first teahouse, a structure built for the sole purpose of serving and drinking tea.

The Japanese Tea Ceremony.

The History and Migration of Tea   23

From East to West:
The Spread of Tea Around the World

1598   The first writing about tea in English appears in the "Voyages and Travels of Hugo Van Linschoten." The author is a Dutch trader who has travelled to the Far East.

1600   Queen Elizabeth I (1533-1603) establishes the East India Company for the well-being of the English Crown. The East India Company, also known as the John Company, will become the largest trading company in the world at that time. It is from learned travellers writing about their journeys in the East that Western countries like England come to know about tea. The British and Continentals already have a passion for Chinese silks, ceramics, and spices.

1610   Green tea begins its migration from East to West. The Dutch traders obtain tea cargo from Macao, an outpost of the advanced Cathay Empire. They purchase the tea from the Portuguese, who are allowed to trade there. The Dutch also bring Yi-Hsing teapots to the Continent.

   The Dutch also win the favor of the Japanese and are allowed trading in Nagasaki. Dutch traders bring Japanese tea back to the Netherlands.

1618   Tea arrives in Russia. It is first brought to Moscow by Chinese ambassadors to the Russian tsar.

1635   While the Chinese have long hailed tea as a medicinal elixir, the Continentals view tea with more skepticism. The Europeans do not accept the divine notion of tea. The first known European to dispute the reputed Chinese attributions to tea is Simon Paulli, a German physician, who publishes a treatise criticizing tea in this year.

1637   Despite its adversaries elsewhere in Europe, tea becomes an established drink of the people in the Netherlands.

1641   A proponent of tea, Dutch physician Nikolas Dirx (pseudonym—Tulp) claims, "Those who use it [tea] are for that reason alone exempt from all maladies and reach an extreme old age."

1658   Tea is about to become popular among the English. It is first served and sold publicly at Thomas Garway's Coffee House in Exchange Alley, London. Until this time, coffee is the most widely consumed hot drink in England. At this time the Ch'ing Dynasty rules China. Some Manchus add milk to their tea. Early travellers to China may well have experienced this custom, and it may have influenced the English's propensity for drinking tea with milk.

1660   Tea is introduced by the Dutch colonists to America in the settlement called New Amsterdam, which will later become New York.

Also in 1660, the first tax on tea in England is levied. The excise tax amounts to eight pence on every gallon of tea sold through the coffeehouses. Taxes on tea will last for over one hundred years.

1664   Charles II of England receives a gift of *thea* from the British East India Company. Charles' consort, Catherine de Braganza from Portugal, having acquired her own knowledge of tea in her homeland, serves tea to the ladies of the English court. Tea very quickly becomes popular with the aristocracy. Tea drinking gains a foothold among the English populace during Charles II's reign.

Debate continues in England, as it does on the Continent, as to whether or not tea has medicinal value. One theory has it that tea, if drunk with pure honey, is good for the kidneys. The same side of the debate believes tea is a panacea for the ills of the spleen, kidneys, heart, lungs, eyes, digestive tract, and gall bladder. And even more, it allegedly could cure fevers and colds. On the other hand, others believe it could cause premature death.

1670   Early English silver teapots are crafted in an attempt to find the perfect tea server.

1680   Tea is brought to Scotland by the Duchess of York, future wife of King James II. She had drunk it in the Netherlands.

By this time in the Netherlands, *t'ay* is being drunk by all classes of people. Women, as customary household hostesses, are now serving tea at home to family and guests. Tea shops serve several types of steeped tea for their customers to taste and assess before purchasing their choices of teas and tea blends. Some Dutch women become tea vendors, selling tea with milk in the streets. They sell tea from a table on which rests a kettle, pitchers of milk, saucers, and other tea utensils. Or they place their "tea things" on wheelbarrows and wheel their fare from street to street. Tea is also being served throughout the country at inns and roadside resting places. It has become the preferred drink of the Dutch at breakfast.

1685 Meanwhile, Emperor K'ang Hsi of China allows the English to spend their money in tea trade with his country. Tea is finally imported directly to England from the Chinese region of Amoy. *T'e* is Amoy dialect for tea. The English intonation becomes "tea."

1689 Now that England is importing tea directly from China, the government realizes tea could be a major commodity with which to gain income for the Crown. Consequently, a very steep tax of five shillings is levied on every pound of dried tea. The result of this tax imposition is dramatic: it leads to 100 years of tea smuggling involving people from all levels of English society. The English find so many ways to import their tea without paying the tax that soon two-thirds of all the tea drunk in England will be smuggled in.

Russia is also expanding her trade relations. She signs a treaty with China, making Kiakhta, a town on the Sino-Russian border, a trade exchange center. Tea is carried to Russia across Manchuria and Mongolia by many camel tea caravans.

1690s While the English and Russians become tea drinkers, the French, on the other hand, are becoming enamored with coffee.

1698 Staffordshire potters make teapots, cups, and saucers of red or brown earthenware as the demand for tea produces a tea-craft industry.

1700s Unlike coffee, which has been hailed as the drink of the creative, tea is not widely seen as having this inspirational property. However, it has been referred to as the drink of the intelligent, owing to its capacity to keep a person awake for long hours, participating in constructive thought. At the same time, tea, like coffee, is considered to be the drink of the sober.

Famous tea drinkers of the time include: William Congreve, William Cowper, Henry Fielding, Samuel Johnson, and Alexander Pope.

The British East India Company becomes the largest trading company in the world. Tea is the company's largest import commodity. Among the teas now being imported to England and the Continent are the black teas—*Bohea* and *Souchong*—and the green teas—*Singlo and Twankay, Gunpowder, and Hyson.*

As a result of this increased trade in teas, the English public is more selective and is now demanding "broken leaf" teas because they infuse faster, proof that time is of the essence, not taste.

THE TEA BOOK

At the same time, some of the wealthy people build private teahouses on the same grounds as their main residences. These early teahouses are usually built with an Oriental design. Also in England, beautiful silver tea equipage is created for the tea industry. Small pear-shaped teapots, tea kettles, cream jugs, and sugar bowls become fashionable.

Not long afterwards, porcelain ware is created in Germany. Breakfast tea sets or *"déjeuner sets"* (tea for two) with porcelain tea trays are finely crafted. It is discovered that the white surface of porcelain is an excellent medium for hand painting decorations on teaware.

1707   Thomas Twining, a weaver, opens Tom's Coffee House in Devereux Court, just off London's Strand Street. The location proves profitable because many of the aristocracy live nearby in the west end of the city. Twining does a very good business using tea as the main attraction to draw customers to his shop.

1716   Tea reaches Hudson Bay in Canada. It will travel with the pioneers in covered wagons to the settlement areas of the Canadian West.

1717   Always on the lookout to increase his business, Thomas Twining sees a new niche in the market. He converts Tom's Coffee House into the first tea shop and calls it "The Golden Lyon." Previously, English coffeehouses had been patronized by men only. Now, Twining invites women to patronize his establishment.

1721   The East India Company is given a monopoly on all teas imported to England.

1730s   Tea has become a prized commodity on the European financial market. Chinese green teas and blended teas are sold at auctions.

1740   Thomas Potter Wheildon (1719-95), one of England's best known potters, founds his factory. An excellent craftsman in experimenting with molds, colored clays, stains, and glazes, he influences many artisans of his time. Among his apprentices are Josiah Spode and Uriah Sutton. Wheildon becomes best known for his cream-colored earthenware with mottled glaze, stained in six colors, referred to as tortoise-shell ware or Wheildon Ware.

1744   In Scotland, some towns and parishes suspect tea of causing serious ailments, and there is even a proposal to jail tea drinkers.

In England, however, tea is now the national drink for all social classes, having gained complete control of the English palate. England is on her way to becoming consummately famous for her tea-drinking customs.

1750 Black teas surpass green teas in imports to the European market.

1754 Thomas Wheildon and Josiah Wedgwood become partners until 1759. Most of the pottery being created in England comes from Staffordshire County, Borough of Stoke-on-Trent, otherwise known as "The Potteries."

House-shaped teapot, Staffordshire, ca. 1740.

Molded teapot in crouching camel shape, Staffordshire, ca. 1745.

1765   Josiah Wedgwood (1730-95) creates a major impact on the ceramics industry. His Queen's Ware (named after Queen Charlotte) is given royal patronage and is mass produced. The new tableware is made of cream-colored earthenware that is resistant to heat. Wedgwood's formula for earthenware sets the standard for teaware.

1767   The British government puts even heavier duties on tea imported to the American colonists. The colonists refuse to pay the tax; instead, they smuggle their tea in from Holland. American colonists' feelings of resistance to British control over them are increasing.

1769   Josiah Wedgwood forms a business partnership with Thomas Bentley (1730-80). The partnership between them is very successful, continuing until Bentley's death. In 1769 Wedgwood and Bentley market Black Basaltes Ware. The Basaltes Ware is made from clay and ground ironstone with manganese and ochre added. Because the ware is so hard, it can be polished on a lapidary wheel, thereby making it conducive to creating busts and medallions as well as tea services.

1773   A British boat with a tea cargo sails into Boston, a colonial hotbed of American resistance to British rule. The colonists refuse to allow the tea, now a symbol of British control and oppression, to be unloaded. The ship's captain, on the other hand, has orders not to leave port until the cargo has been discharged. American colonists decide to oblige the captain's orders. Dressed as Mohawk Indians, several colonists secretly board the ship at night and unload the 342 chests of green tea into the cool waters of the Boston Harbor. The stand-off ends in what will forever be known as the most famous tea party in history, "The Boston Tea Party" (December 16, 1773).

1774   Forever the experimenter, Josiah Wedgwood develops Jasper Ware, a white vitrified stoneware. It is the Jasper Ware, particularly, the blue and white ware with its cameo reliefs, that the name Wedgwood will become synonymous with. He becomes the only English potter of that time to gain an international market and to become well known on the Continent.

1779   Wedgwood goes on to develop his cream-colored Queen's Ware further by putting a cobalt-blue-tinted glaze over it. The result is a white pearly-like hue; thus Pearl-Ware is born. Pearl-Ware is created mainly for tea services to rival the continental porcelain.

1780s In England, while the people are not as openly rebellious to the tea tax as are the American colonists, the English try to avoid the high taxes on tea by blending together different varieties of tea leaves. In fact, many businessmen get their start as tea blenders. Harrod's of London and Cadbury's ("The Milk-Chocolate People") were originally tea blenders. Smugglers decide to get involved in the "blending" too. They adulterate the tea because the demand for it is higher than the quantity being imported. Such tea bulkers as sloe and elder buds are added to tea to puff up the quantity sold and to pump up the pocketbooks of these tea "entrepreneurs." Tea is even being mixed with leaves from the poisonous ash tree.

1784   Richard Twining, grandson of Thomas Twining, persuades British Prime Minister William Pitt to drop the taxes on tea to businesses and to substitute a set fee paid only by the tea companies to the Crown annually. The fee is not to be passed on to consumers. Following Twining's advice, Prime Minister Pitt attacks the smuggling problem by eliminating tea taxes, thereby lowering the price of tea to consumers and making tea smuggling unprofitable. The solution creates unemployment as it dries up the lifeblood of many an English "free enterpriser."

Tea consumption in Britain rises significantly after the tax is removed. The increasing British demand for tea affects the world trade picture. The British grow more opium in India, and the traders smuggle it into China to decrease their payments for tea. In the past, China has accepted only silver as payment for tea and this drain of silver has been hard on the British currency exchange. As the British tea traders smuggle opium into China, many Chinese people are becoming addicted to the drug.

1800s   In Holland, *t'ay* is widely sold in apothecary shops. A common daily drink among the populace, it is still considered medicinal there. Meanwhile, in England, tea gardens spring up on the outskirts of towns and villages. The gardens provide settings for family outings. In addition to tea, sandwiches and pastries are served. The tea gardens are patronized by men, women, and children.

1823   The English, like the Dutch, are constantly searching for new sources of tea. British Army Maj. Robert Bruce visits the mountainous jungle regions of Assam, where he finds scores of wild tea plants.

1824   The first tea from China is planted in the botanical gardens at Peradeniya, Ceylon.

1825   In North America, the building of the Erie Canal, from New York to the Great Lakes, will affect tea trade around the world. American merchants order the building of the fastest trading ships in the world—the clippers. The name comes from the phrase "moving at a good clip," as the clippers can "clip" time from long ocean voyages. The huge ships will soon transport enormous amounts of the precious tea cargo to market and America and England will begin speed-sailing them in record times around the world as they race to get their tea to market.

1826   A new feature in the tea trade is introduced. Englishman John Horniman sells tea in sealed packages. He also develops a machine to produce packages that will hold larger quantities of tea.

1830   Tea finds a new supporter from an unusual source. The Industrial Revolution has added to the problem of alcoholism, and the urban streets of England are filled with drunken men. With "Tea and God on their side," members of the Temperance Movement (founded in 1818) find a way to bring salvation to the many lost souls. Tea, the temperers claim, "will help to keep gentlemen sober and out of hell."

1833   As the story goes, if it is at all correct, a drunk named Dickie Turner stumbles upon a Temperance meeting somewhere in Preston, England. Completely taken up by their doctrine at this one meeting, the still somewhat intoxicated Turner screams out, "I'll reet down and tee total forever and ever." He gains his sobriety and the English vocabulary gains a new word—"teetotaling."

The search for new sources of tea continues. Jacobus Isidorus Lodewijk Leujen (J. I. L. L.) Jacobson, a Dutchman, smuggles tea seeds and teamen out of China. On his last voyage from China, and faced with a price on his head levied by the Chinese, Jacobson barely escapes. Chased by Mandarins over the seas, he makes it to Java with millions of tea seeds and fifteen teamen.

In spite of this illustrious effort at smuggling, the planting of the tea seeds in Java fails. Chinese tea does not grow well in Indonesian soil. Finally, tea seeds from Assam in India are brought to Java. Assam seeds are more suited to the soil of the Malay archipelago and their cultivation is successful.

1834   Because of the English concern over the shortage of tea sources, Governor-General Lord William Cavendish Bentinck appoints the first Tea Committee to investigate whether tea can be grown in India. The Committee reports back that tea can be successfully cultivated in Assam. As a result of the Committee's findings, the popular belief that the best tea can only come from China is being rethought by the English.

Charles Bruce, Robert Bruce's brother, seeds the hillsides of Darjeeling in northern India with wild tea plants. As a result of these experiments, the Darjeeling region will later produce some of the finest teas in the world.

1836   Two brothers, Edward and Joseph Tetley, sell tea and salt on horseback to the farmers and villagers of Yorkshire. Joseph Tetley & Company Ltd. is founded as a tea-packing house.

1837   Twining receives a Royal Warrant from Queen Victoria. Since then, the Royal Family of England have continued their patronage of Twining, allowing the logo of the Royal Coat of Arms to be displayed on their tea packages.

1838   The British government annexes Assam. They are planning on getting into the tea venture in a big way.

1839   Charles Bruce, who is in charge of the English efforts to grow tea in Assam, India, finally sends the promised reward in the form of eight chests of tea to the London auction. This tea symbolizes for the English their own capacity for growing tea.

1840   Anna, the Duchess of Bedford, creates the afternoon teatime. The underclasses get word of this new practice among the aristocracy. The ritual of an afternoon tea quickly catches on among the masses and it soon becomes institutionalized within the British way of life.

1841   Tea seeds are sent to the Rothschild Coffee Estate in Ceylon. The planting is for experimental purposes only. In the coming years, starting in 1869, the first plant disease known to coffee plantations in the world strikes in Ceylon. The disease is rust fungus *(Hemileia vasterix)*. In the following years, the Ceylon coffee plantations are infested and wiped out. Tea estates begin to be developed in their place.

1842   Known as the First Opium War, a war between China and England is fought. The war begins after an English sailor is killed in a fight. When the English win the war with all their modern artillery, China agrees to open up more ports to foreign ships. Thus Britain gains control of her tea markets. By the treaty of Nanking, Hong Kong is ceded to Britain by China. The British stranglehold on tea exporting continues. More and more Chinese people become addicted to opium.

1843   Back in Britain, people employed in the ale industry are losing their jobs as the nation takes up tea drinking. The economic difficulties experienced by England are blamed on tea. As a result, many people are broadcasting information on the addictive quality of tea.

1851   Tea grown in Assam, India (by this time under British colonial control) is on display at London's "Great Exhibition"—the world's first International Fair. The British make it known to the world how successful they are with their tea-growing venture. Along with their "tea pride," the British also become very grumpy and edgy if their tea is in short supply.

1854   The British bring tea to Morocco. Eventually, Morocco becomes a major tea-drinking nation.

1866   The Greatest Tea Clipper Race in history (from Foochow to London) takes place. This is perhaps the tightest clipper-ship race in history. The *Taeping* docks in London first, winning the race by only twenty minutes over the *Ariel*. The ships, in a neck-and-neck race, have taken only 102 days to travel three-quarters of the way around the world.

1870s   The clipper ships decline in use with the development of faster steamships.

1878   Tea is cultivated in Malawi (formerly Nyasaland), the first African country to develop tea estates. Malawi spreads tea to other East African countries.

1880s   Thomas Lipton buys tea plantations in Ceylon, and thanks to his strong business sense, within the decade Ceylon begins to develop into a major tea-producing country.

1884   The idea for Joseph Lyons' involvement in tea comes from Montague Gluckstein, a travelling tobacco salesman. Gluckstein found it difficult to find refreshments "on the road." Lyons joins with him and becomes chairman of a non-alcoholic catering business.

1887   Lyons and Gluckstein put a bid into the Newcastle Exhibition to sell fresh tea to visitors for two pence a pot, instead of the usual cup of overbrewed tea, which at the time was sold to the public for three pence (the saying "tea for two," meaning tea for a two-pence, originates from this). Their contract is accepted and Joseph Lyons & Company launches into the tea business.

1894   The first Lyons Tea Shop opens in Piccadilly in the heart of London. This shop still exists today.

1897   The United States Tea Act is passed to ensure improved standards for tea imports. The legislation protects consumers from inferior-grade teas and tea leaves that have been adulterated with other ingredients.

1898   Tea is introduced to Iran. It will later be grown near the Caspian Sea.

1900s Other companies get on the tea bandwagon. A manageress with the English Aerated Bread Company begins to serve tea to her favorite customers, in the back room of her bread shop. The service is so well received that patrons return time and time again. The Company decides to open up a tea shop. The A.B.C., as it is known to the English, eventually develops the largest chain of tea shops in England.

Tea shops become a respectable bastion for women, enabling them to share tea and their secrets in private. Herein, cups of cheer and cups of gloom and doom are shared.

By now J. Lyons Tea Shop has over 250 outlets. The waitresses are called "nippies" because they nip around from table to table serving tea and snacks.

A company called The Brothers Neal Stationers begins to serve tea and biscuits in their shop. Tea as a "meal" outside the home is born. Eventually The Brothers Neal Stationers become W. H. Smith and Sons' Tea Rooms.

In England, tea dances are popular. These are tea parties where debutantes and gentlemen meet at five o'clock in the afternoon at their favorite hotel. An orchestra would play and the participants would pass away the hours drinking tea and dancing. The dances started in the early 1900s and sadly they ended in 1939, as a result of all the men having to leave for the war.

In China, the empress dowager, leader of the Ch'ing Dynasty, is fearful of foreign powers. She pressures a group of Mandarins to attempt a massacre of foreigners living in the Legation Quarters of Peking. The Mandarins try and fail. World powers withdraw their trade from China. Only Twining will remain a trading partner with China, as she sinks into further isolation from the rest of the world.

1900   Tea is planted in the botanical gardens at Entebbe, Uganda, where it is still grown.

1903   Tea seeds from India are planted near Limuru, near Nairobi, Kenya. Later, many of Kenya's teas will be used in tea blends and exported to over forty countries.

1904 American iced tea is invented at the St. Louis World's Fair. With the temperature climbing to over 104 degrees, a tea promoter named Richard Blechynden is having difficulty selling his hot tea to an already sweating crowd of spectators. Looking for a gimmick, he dumps ice into the tea and serves up a new "thirst quencher."

1906 Okakura Kakuzo, a university scholar in Japan, writes *The Book of Tea* to introduce the West to the Japanese Tea Ceremony and the history of tea in Japan.

1908 The tea bag is born as an accident. American tea importer Thomas Sullivan wants to reduce the expense of sending tea to his customers in tins. He decides to send them tea samples in tiny silk bags, as gifts. His customers, not knowing what to do with them, place them in their teapots, add hot water, and steep the tea.

"The Baker's Shoppe" collector's teapot and teacup with a tea cozy.

The History and Migration of Tea

1914-18 Leaders of the British wartime effort find that they can increase their workers' productivity by giving them a supply of tea to get them through the day. Tea also accompanies soldiers to war as part of their rations.

1925 The Brooke Bond Company begins cultivating tea in the Highlands of Kericho in Kenya. Tea estates in Africa will eventually produce high-grade teas, known for their blending qualities and full-bodied tastes.

1940s Tea is cultivated in Turkey.

1950 Sositsu Sen, the fifteenth Grand Tea Master of the *Urasenke* School of Tea in Japan, devotes his time to spreading *chado,* "the way of tea," abroad. The *Urasenke* School of Tea was begun by a grandson of Sen-no Rikyu. There are two other prominent schools teaching the Tea Ceremony in Japan, the *Mushanokojisenke* and the *Omete Senke,* both also begun by Sen-no Rikyu's grandsons.

1952 The tea rationing that began in England during World War II finally ends. Tea sales increase dramatically.

1953 The Tetley Tea Company introduces the paper tea bag to the mass British market. The tea-bag phenomenon will change tea-drinking habits around the world. The Tetley Tea Company will become known to consumers through their unique and full-fledged advertising campaign as "The Teabag People."

1956 Instant tea mixes were not created accidentally as were some of the other innovations in tea's history. The Nestle Company and Standard Brands (manufacturer of Tender Leaf Teas) worked for years to develop a water-soluble tea.

In the same year, The Tea Cub, Britain's first automatic tea machine, is manufactured by W. H. Smith & Sons Ltd. It is promoted to be used in offices.

1973 Lyons buys the Tetley Tea Company to establish themselves under the name of Lyons Tetley Ltd. They become the largest tea company in the world.

1989 Lyons Tetley Ltd. markets the Round Tea Bag. Each bag, they boast, has 2,000 perforations for full flavor to flood through.

1990s Canned iced tea in aluminum soda cans is sold in grocery outlets across the United States. Fruit-flavored iced teas are soon sold in bottles to compete with soda. The new marketing of iced tea as a thirst quencher appeals to younger people and the sports-minded.

The Commonwealth countries, due to their former affiliation with Britain as colonies or protectorates, remain the largest group of tea-producing countries in the world.

2000 Research into the effects of green tea on the human body will confirm that this tea is healthy for us. A huge revival of drinking green tea will occur throughout the Western world. Tea perhaps may then be viewed as it was first seen by the ancients . . . a divine drink.

British Teatimes

Many countries around the world have their own special "teatimes," customary occasions when they enjoy drinking tea. However, perhaps nowhere in the world does the word "teatime" ring a bell as it does in England.

During the last three centuries, the English have created specific times and special places where tea is to be served and enjoyed. To the rest of the world, the British obsession with their tea and teatimes has become well noted. Some of these well-known "teas" are described in the following pages.

Breakfast Tea

By the 1700s, tea for breakfast had become indoctrinated into the English lifestyle. It replaced the customary practice of drinking ale at breakfast.

The institution of tea for breakfast was probably most influenced by Queen Anne (1665-1714). In fact, so well known was Queen Anne for her liking of tea that Alexander Pope (1688-1744), satirist of the day, mocked:

> Here thou, great Anna! whom three realms obey,
> Dost sometimes counsel take—and sometimes tea.
> (*The Rape of the Lock,* London, 1712-14)

Suggested Teas: English Breakfast Tea, Irish Breakfast Tea, Ceylon Breakfast Tea. These are strong blends of teas from India and Ceylon, each with that little extra amount of caffeine to help kick off the morning.

Suggested Tea Accompaniments: quick breads with herbs, toast and butter, waffles.

Low Tea (Afternoon Tea—4:00 P.M.)

Low tea may have begun with the Duchess Anna of Bedford, around 1840. Feeling faint in the afternoons (probably from hypoglycemia), she started sipping tea to get her through to the very late seven o'clock English dinner. Soon after, she began serving "tea and snacks" to her aristocratic friends in the afternoon. When the public got word of the aristocracy's new practice, they too began sitting down for the ritual of afternoon tea.

Later, Queen Victoria (1819-1901) further popularized this teatime by sitting down herself to tea every day in the afternoon. During her reign, Charles Dickens (1812-70) described the "institution of afternoon tea" in *Barnaby Rudge*. He depicted the moment when all of England sits down to tea as one "in which we are perfectly contented with ourselves and one another."

Suggested Teas: Ceylon teas, Earl Grey, Darjeeling, Tea with a Twist, Chinese Gunpowder, Dragonwell.

Suggested Tea Accompaniments: bread and butter, cakes, fruit tarts, macaroons, dainty sandwiches.

High Tea (6:00 P.M.)

The poor working class of England created the ritual called "high tea." Since the poor could only afford one solid meal a day, which was usually lunch, more often than not workers returned home in the evening tired and hungry.

High tea started with just a pot o' tea around six o'clock in the evening to tide one over until the next day's meal. Sometimes it was accompanied by leftovers that could be pocketed during the day from the serving of the middle classes' lunch. Bread and cheese, cold meats, sausages—anything that could be tucked away was brought home to add a little sustenance to the tea.

Eventually, as the wealth of the nation increased and the number of people in the middle class grew, high tea developed into a more substantial light meal that included cooked portions such as eggs, sausages, fish, and mashed potatoes. Nowadays, high tea is no longer needed, having been replaced with a dinner. Tea, however, is still enjoyed after the evening meal.

Suggested Teas: Ceylon blended teas, Assam blended teas.

Suggested Tea Accompaniments: biscuits or scones with jam, cheese or meats, light meals (e.g., eggs and sausages with French fries and peas).

Tea Break

This is a period of fifteen minutes to one-half hour in midmorning and midafternoon, designed for those in the working force to cease work activities and relax for a few minutes with cups of tea. Cookies, or "biscuits," are often served at tea-break time.

The concept of a tea break got its start over 250 years ago when some employers served tea in the morning to their employees who began work at five or six o'clock. At that time, the tea break was highly controversial and many employers were against the practice because they thought it would only serve to make their employees lazy or—worse—lazier.

Tea breaks received more official recognition during World War I, when employers realized they could increase the productivity and stamina of their employees by giving them a supply of tea to get through the day. The practice continued and spread to other work settings after the war.

Nowadays, most Westerners in the work force take tea or coffee breaks for granted. Many labor unions have midmorning and midafternoon breaks written into their labor contracts and some labor codes require the break.

Suggested Teas: Earl Grey, Lapsang Souchong, Orange Pekoe grade teas.

Suggested Tea Accompaniments: shortbreads, sugar cookies, quick breads (zucchini bread, oatcakes).

Nursery Tea or Tea-Party Time

In the midmorning and midafternoon, English children being cared for in nurseries cease their play activities to gather together for milky cups of tea and biscuits. The tea break is often referred to by English children as "tea-party time." Nursery rhymes about tea have been created to entertain children. Two of the most well known are:

> I'm a little teapot, short and stout—
> Here is my handle; here is my spout.
> I'm a little teapot, short and stout—
> Tip me over and pour me out.

> Twinkle, twinkle, little bat!
> How I wonder what you're at!
> Up above the world you fly,
> Like a teatray in the sky.
>
> —Lewis Carroll, *Alice in Wonderland*

Suggested Teas: Cambric Tea, Vanilla Nursery Tea.

Suggested Tea Accompaniments: tea biscuits, cinnamon rolls, jam cookies, oatcakes.

Summer Tea at the Tea Gardens

Tea gardens originally sprang up on the outskirts of cities in England. The tea gardens provided an excellent environment for relaxed family outings. Families could take a stroll around the lawns and gardens, admire the flowers, then sip tea, eat dainty sandwiches, and chat.

Nowadays tea gardens are still enjoyed by men, women, and children. Sunday, the Christian day of rest, is viewed as a fitting time to take in an afternoon teatime—at a tea garden.

Suggested Teas: Darjeeling, Earl Grey.

Suggested Tea Accompaniments: cucumber, egg, ham, or watercress sandwiches (crusts removed); whipped red salmon in bread rolls; slices from cream-cheese loaves; tea cakes; fresh berry tarts.

Strawberry Tea/Spring Tea

June in many countries is strawberry month, so strawberry teas occur in the late springtime. They are sometimes held by charitable organizations as fund-raisers. Guests are offered a choice of scrumptious desserts along with the customarily served strawberry shortcake dripping with thick or whipped cream.

Suggested Teas: *Queen Mary Tea Blend:* "a special blend of broken orange teas which Twining personally supplied to the late Queen Mary of England" (according to Twining's "Capture the Moment with Twining Tea: A Connoisseur's Guide").

Prince of Wales Tea: "a leafy, bright liquoring tea exclusively blended and sold by Twining and considered the 'Burgundy of China Teas.' This tea variety is grown in the Anhwei Province of China" (same source).

Earl Grey: "one of the most popular blended teas. The favorite of the British Prime Minister, Earl Grey, this blend was presented to him in 1830, and has been named for him since. Earl Grey is a subtle blend of oil of Bergamot, a citrus fruit from Italy, and Chinese and Indian black teas" (The Stash Tea Company). Jackson of Piccadilly claims to have created the Earl Grey tea blend for Earl Grey.

Suggested Tea Accompaniments: strawberry shortcake with thick Devonshire cream, cream-cheese pies, trifles, meringues. Garnish tea with strawberry slices or serve tea with strawberries on the side.

Tea-Shop Tea

In 1774, the first Lyons tea shop opened in Piccadilly, London. By 1900, Lyons had over 250 outlets throughout England. Here a cup could be shared while patrons reflected on the sentiment of Shelley when he wrote:

Teas
where small talk dies in agonies.

Today, tea-shop tea remains popular in England, where one can partake in "tea and tidbits."

Suggested Teas: Ceylon teas, Assam teas (Orange Pekoe grade).

Suggested Tea Accompaniments: scones and butter, tea biscuits, crumpets.

Hotel Tea

In the 1700s in England, roadside inns began serving tea by the fireplace as a warm way to greet weary travellers. Later, many hotels offered their own tea and trappings for their clientele. The tradition continues today as many hotels and roadside inns have special teatimes.

England has a large dairy industry and the English indulge often in their high-cholesterol favorite—cream. They differentiate between double cream, heavy cream, single cream, and cream, loving desserts with one of the above included. The roadside inns in England are famous for their teas slopping with cream. Urbanites like to travel to the country on weekends to take in a roadside inn teatime.

Suggested Teas: a wide variety of teas for guests to experience tea blends from around the world—Russian Caravan, Lapsang Souchong, Orange Spiced, Chinese scented teas.

Suggested Tea Accompaniments: dainty sandwiches and regal desserts such as scones bathed in thick clotted cream.

Tea at the Ritz

One of the world's most renowned hotel teas is the afternoon tea at London's opulent Hotel Ritz. César Ritz, a onetime waiter there, referred to his namesake as "the most famous hotel in the most fashionable city in the world." The Ritz, which has been serving tea to London society since it first opened in 1906, was the first hotel in London to allow ladies in unescorted.

Today the "Tea at the Ritz" is still formal, but not stuffy. There was a time, however, when anybody who thought he/she was a somebody wanted to be seen either going into or coming out of the Ritz.

The present-day menu includes finger sandwiches of cucumber and anchovies, egg mayonnaise with mustard and watercress, and meat such as ham, smoked salmon, or smoked turkey with sweet mustard. Warm scones are still served covered with strawberry jam and clotted cream.

Teatime Is Anytime

Teatime is anytime in England. The English preoccupation with tea drinking is reflected well by Dr. Samuel Johnson, critic, journalist, author, and noted conversationalist (1709-84). In *A Review of "A Journal of Eighty Days"* (*Literary Magazine,* London, 1757), Dr. Johnson proudly described himself as "a hardened and shameless tea-drinker, who has for twenty years diluted his meals with only the infusion of this fascinating plant; whose kettle has scarcely time to cool; who with tea amuses the evening, with tea solaces the midnight, and with tea welcomes the morning."

Tea-Leaf Reading

Matrons, who toss the cup, and see
The grounds of fate in grounds of tea . . .

—Alexander Pope

Tea-leaf reading is the study of the configurations formed by the wet tea leaves on the interior walls of a teacup, after the tea has been drunk. This study of the tea-leaf configurations is also referred to as *tasseography,* which means the reading of a map in the cup.

Tea-leaf readers draw upon a wide variety of symbols to conceptualize their readings. The symbols that teacup diviners utilize are derived from almost every identifiable object found in our earth's environment. Trees (sturdy or weak), clouds (heavy or light), birds (eagles or vultures), or flowers (with those wonderful human qualities man has attributed to them) provide meaning for the reader in the interpretation of the cup.

Teacup readers also make use of interpretations and symbols from some of the world's more ancient studies, such as astrology and numerology. A teacup

45

reader can draw on as many symbols and studies as he/she considers useful to do a teacup reading.

The process of teacup reading begins with the fate seeker drinking a straight infusion of tea, preferably made from tea leaves. In preparing tea for a teacup reading, the usual instructions for making tea are sufficient. A teacup strainer, however, should not be used, as the object of a teacup reading is to read one's fortune from the tea-leaf configurations that are left in the cup, after the tea has been consumed.

Next the reader will turn the emptied teacup around three times in a counterclockwise direction with his/her left hand. Then the fate seeker will turn the cup over onto a saucer and, taking his/her left hand and placing it on top of the upside-down cup, turn it three times in a counterclockwise direction. The tea drinker makes sure the handle of the teacup ends up facing the reader. By laying his/her hand on top of the upside-down cup, the fate seeker adds his/her energy or "aura" to the teacup.

When this is done, the reader turns the teacup over, making sure not to shake or move the tea-leaf configurations that have formed on the interior wall of the teacup. The reader studies the leaves, identifying the symbols they have formed. He/she will probably view the cup from as many different angles or directions as possible.

Next comes the real magic of a teacup reading. The reader incorporates his/her instinctual, physical, and psychic senses into the interpretation of what he/she "sees" in the cup. A good reader will be able to identify the formations in relation to each other. Then he/she will piece together the meanings represented by the symbols into a full interpretation for the fate seeker to understand.

Configurations that are located within a quarter-inch of each other are generally considered together. It is believed that they most likely influence each other. Some formations are interpreted literally by the reader; others are interpreted symbolically. A configuration that does not resemble any form known to the reader is read by instinct, and related to the rest of the symbols in the cup. All tea-leaf formations are considered vital to the overall reading.

Significant also to the teacup reading is the position in which the tea-leaf configurations are found, as they indicate a geographic location, a time period, and whether friends, family, or strangers will be involved in future events in the life of the fate seeker. Tea-leaf formations closest to the handle represent the fate seeker's home area and family occurrences. Configurations directly opposite this area, on the far side of the cup across from the handle, represent the life of the fate seeker away from the home area and the effect that strangers may have on his/her life. To the right side of the handle, the tea-leaf formations represent events or people coming into the fate seeker's life. Configurations found on the left side of the handle represent events and people leaving the life of the fate seeker.

THE TEA BOOK

Regarding the timing of events, formations found near the brim of the teacup represent events that will occur in the near future. Symbols found near the bottom represent happenings in the farther-off future, usually in about one year's time from the date of the reading. Configurations near the brim also symbolize the beginning of a month. Those found in the middle represent midmonth and those set near the bottom represent the month's end.

Time is also indicated by where the leaf formations are situated in the overall circumference of the cup. Configurations found 90 degrees left of the handle represent a three-month period into the future. A six-month future period is represented by formations directly opposite the handle. Nine months into the future is represented at 270 degrees. Events taking place at the end of one year from the date of the teacup reading are represented at the full circumference, or approximately 360 degrees in the cup, ending on the right side of the handle. The teacup is always read in a clockwise direction, beginning on the left side of the handle. The handle itself represents the fate seeker.

Tea leaves illuminate the fate seeker's future emotional state as well. The happiest events will be shown in configurations near the rim of the cup. If tea leaves are found at the bottom, a future event may very well affect the fate seeker in a sad way for a time. Leaves situated between the rim and bottom show the normal range of emotional responses to life, from high to low.

Teacup readings are not only done to give insight and guidance. Some are provided by diviners to answer a question put forward by a fate seeker. When doing an inquiry reading, the teacup reader will utilize all of the formations in relation to one question being asked. With this type of reading, the cup will not be used at all for a present or future prophetic reading.

It is important to note that all interpretative readings should be passed on by the reader to the fate seeker in a constructive and nonthreatening way. Consideration of the fate seeker must always be the utmost priority for the reader. The seeker may well remember the essence of a reading for many years to come.

Fate seekers, too, must have appropriate expectations from tea-leaf readings. Even the most accurate or caring reader cannot live out another person's life, nor can a reader provide step-by-step advice on how another person should direct him/herself through life's passages or circumstances. It must be remembered by those persons who are seeking fortune-telling through the teacup that whatever the reading, each person is in charge of his/her own life.

The hostess (teishu) is stirring koicha (a thick tea) with a bamboo whisk (chasen) in a bowl (chawan). On the floor to her left is the water jar (mizusashi) and tea caddy (cha-ire). On the wall is the shifuku (silk cloth cover of the tea caddy). To the hostess's right is the cover to the kettle (kama), resting on a stand (futaoki). The water ladle (hishaku) is resting on the kettle. The kettle is set on the hearth (ro).

Ochaji
(The Japanese Tea Ceremony)

Tea has always had a religious significance among the Japanese. In A.D. 727, Emperor Shomu invited monks to his palace at Nara, offering them a drink of the *ch'a* that he had received as a gift from the T'ang Court in China. Later, in 794, tea seeds were brought to Japan from China. Emperor Kammu planted the seeds at his Imperial Gardens at Heian (Kyoto) and within a few years tea became the drink of the aristocracy and the monks.

However, tea's assimilation into the Japanese culture was to be temporarily halted for, during the next four centuries, Japan became embroiled in civil wars and ties with China were severed. When the wars finally ceased, contact with China was renewed by the ruling Minamota family of Nara (Kyoto area). As the renewal began, China was experiencing the Sung Dynasty (960-1280).

The Chinese culture during the Sung Dynasty was viewed as the most civilized and advanced in the world. It was idolized by the Japanese, who had always emulated the Chinese in as many ways as possible.

In 1191, Japan sent Eisai, a monk scholar, to China. At this time, the Ch'an Buddhist sect in China was developing a ritual of gathering in front of an image of Bodhidharma, a Buddhist saint, while drinking tea from the same bowl. When Eisai returned, he brought with him the knowledge of Zen Buddhism and some tea seeds. These seeds were planted in Uji, near Kyoto, thus beginning tea's cultivation in Japan.

Eisai went on to write the first book on tea drinking ever written in Japan. Through this book, *Kissa Yoyoki* ("Maintaining of One's Health through Drinking Tea"), he influenced the people of Japan to drink the beverage. Eisai believed that it was good for the health of both one's body and mind, and that it would be good for the Japanese people.

In earlier days, it was only the monks of Japan who had access to tea. However, occasionally the monks would hold a charity day, sometimes inviting the poorer people to come to the temples to drink tea. It was at the temples that many people in Japan were introduced to tea. And because the monks prized the tea so much, the people soon wanted what the monks had. Tea became viewed as a symbol of purity, for its qualities of simplicity and meditativeness.

During this period in history, the simple, Zen-influenced tea ceremony became more and more formalized and ritualized. Special rooms were added to houses for the sole purpose of serving tea.

In 1477, Shogun Ashikaga-Yoshimasa employed a Buddhist priest named Shuko specifically to serve tea in a ceremonial fashion at the palace near Kyoto. In his occupation as Tea Master, Shuko developed the "Rules for the Tea Ceremony."

Eventually, every aspect of the tea ritual, from the setting of the teahouse amidst nature's beauty to the actual serving of tea, took on an increasingly significant and symbolic meaning. Finally, in the sixteenth century, Sen-no Rikyu, a monk working for the shogun Toyotomi-Hideyoshi (1536-98), perfected the rules to the Tea Ceremony. For his dedication, Rikyu is remembered and respected by the Japanese as the greatest of their Tea Masters.

The supreme importance of tea to the Japanese is described later by a Japanese university scholar, Okakura Kakuzo (1862-1913), in his work *The Book of Tea* (1906):

> Tea provides a situation, a quiet and peaceful environment for a man to meditate. Teaism is the discipline of the mind, body, heart and spirit. [It] is a cult founded on the adoration of the beautiful among the sordid facts of everyday existence. It inculcates purity and harmony, the mystery of mutual charity, the romanticism of the social order. It is essentially a worship of the Imperfect, as it is a tender attempt to accomplish something possible in this impossible thing we know as life.

The Ceremony

Ochaji (the Tea Ceremony with a light meal) begins with the *shotaijo,* an invitation to the house of the *teishu,* host/ess of the ceremony, and ends with the leaving of the last *kyaku,* guest.

Invitations are mailed to the *kyaku* by the *teishu.* The purpose for the Tea Ceremony is always stated on the *shotaijo.* Ceremonies are held in honor of special events such as religious holidays and for personal celebrations such as birthdays or anniversaries.

The number of persons invited to a ceremony will depend on the size of the *teishu*'s tearoom. One to perhaps twelve persons may be invited. There are larger ceremonies held in Japan with guests numbering thirty people or more.

At the beginning of the ceremony, each *kyaku* will first perform *zenrei*, which is going to the home of the *teishu* one day before the *Ochaji,* to show appreciation and to give thanks to the *teishu* for the invitation to a ceremony. Each guest will not chat or stay for long during this visit because he/she knows the *teishu* is busy preparing for the ceremony. In *Ochaji,* both the *teishu* and the *kyaku* have defined responsibilities to carry out.

On the day of the ceremony, the guests arrive wearing attractive, but acceptable apparel. Their clothing should be clean and neat, and not too showy or obtrusive. It is important not to draw attention away from the Tea Ceremony.

A *shokyaku,* a main guest, has usually been chosen and invited by the *teishu.* It is necessary for the *shokyaku* to have had previous experiences with the Tea Ceremony so that he/she can perform his/her ceremonial duties properly. If a main guest has not been specifically invited by the *teishu,* when the *kyaku* arrive they will choose a *shokyaku* among themselves. Throughout the ceremony, the *shokyaku* will be the spokesperson to the *teishu* on behalf of all the other guests.

When all the guests have arrived at the *yoritsuki,* the waiting room of the *teishu*'s house, they may be met by a *hanto,* a person selected by the *teishu* to aid in the carrying out of the duties of the Tea Ceremony. The *hanto* will offer *yu,* heated water, to the guests while they are waiting. After the guests have sipped a small quantity of water, enough only to moisten their throats, the *hanto* will lead the guests out to the *niwa,* the garden.

In the *niwa* is a *koshikake,* a bench with cushions on it. All of the guests will sit on the *koshikake* and wait for the arrival of their *teishu.* Once all of the guests have arrived, the *teishu* will come to the garden gate and greet the guests in silence, then return to the house. One by one in single file, all the guests will now travel down a *roji,* a special pathway built through the *niwa.* As the guests walk along the pathway, each is expected to communicate silently with nature, for here in the garden is presented for them the perfection and harmony of nature. The journey provides guests with the opportunity to forget about their worldly cares. It is essential for the *teishu* to water the garden one day before and on the morning of the ceremony. Fresh droplets of water on the greenery and flowers in the garden indicate to the guests that the *teishu* has prepared well for their arrival.

Near the end of the pathway is placed a *tsukubai,* an earthenware water basin. One by one each guest stops at the *tsukubai,* washes his/her hands, and rinses out his/her mouth with fresh water from the basin. In washing, the guests follow the etiquette of the Japanese purification rites. First a person washes the left hand, then the right hand. The ladle is dipped again into the water basin and the guest will quietly rinse out his/her mouth with a small amount of water. Symbolically, the washing means the cleansing of the heart and the body. All of the dust and dirt from the outer world are washed away.

At the end of the journey through the garden, the guests will enter in single file the *chashitsu,* the tearoom, through a *nijiriguchi,* a three-foot-high sliding door.

They enter in a crouching position. The lowering of the body symbolizes an expression of humility, which the guests adopt as they are about to join the ceremony. Social class does not matter in the Tea Ceremony; all of the guests are considered to be equal.

The last guest to enter the tearoom will close the door with an emphatic gesture, making sure the sound of the door closing can be heard. This indicates to the *teishu* that all the invited guests are now within the tearoom. One by one the guests will go to the *tokonoma,* the alcove that is the place of "most honor" in the tearoom. Here each person will kneel, placing in front of oneself a fan that each has brought along to the ceremony. The guests will admire a *chabana,* a flower arrangement, and a *kakemono,* a hanging scroll, which has been set out for them to admire by the *teishu.* The *chabana* symbolizes the season in nature when the particular ceremony is being held. For example, if a ceremony is being held in April, the arrangement will have an appropriate spring flower in it, such as the cherry blossom. The *kakemono* will have calligraphic lettering on it stating the reason for the ceremony. The Japanese love the Tea Ceremony, so they have created an abundance of reasons for having it.

Ceremonies may be held for birthdays, graduations, good-bye parties (if relatives are going abroad), and welcome-back parties (when relatives return from abroad). There are specific ceremonies paying tribute to each of the changing seasons and to almost every month in the year. Examples of some of these celebrations are New Year's (January), Buddha's Birthday (April), Boy's Day (May), the beginning of summer (June), the Star Festival (July), and the Kimona Festival (August).

After admiring the *chabana* and the *kakemono,* the guests move on to the *ro,* a fire hearth. The hearth will be recessed into the floor, if the ceremony is taking place in the wintertime. During the summer months of May to November, a *furo,* a ceramic hearth above ground, is used for the heating of the tea water.

At the hearth, each guest will inspect the *kama* (iron kettle) that sits on the fire. They will then turn to a shelf by the hearth and admire the *kogo,* an incense burner set on it. Below the shelf, on the floor, the *teishu* will have set out the *mizusashi,* a ceramic water jar, and the *cha-ire,* the tea caddy, for the guests to view.

After paying tribute to all of these, the main guest will go and seat him/herself on a *tatami,* a rice straw mat on the tearoom floor. Following his/her example, one by one the other guests will sit down in a row. Tearooms are covered with rice straw mats. Each *tatami* measures three feet by six feet and is meant to accommodate one seated person.

Once everyone is seated, the *teishu* enters the tearoom and bows to the guests. The teishu and guests exchange greetings. The *teishu* then returns to the *mizuya,* the preparation room, where he/she retrieves the *sumitori,* a basket containing charcoal, in order to perform the *Shozumi,* the First Charcoal Ceremony. Back in the tearoom, the *teishu* adds and arranges the *sumi,* charcoals, in the fire to make it strong for the heating of the tea water. During the *Shozumi,* the *teishu* will also place *ko,* incense, in the fire. The type of incense used is matched with the various seasons of the year. For example, April brings the blooming of the cherry trees in Japan, so cherry-blossom incense would be appropriate for an April Tea Ceremony.

While the *teishu* is placing the incense in the fire, the main guest may ask the *teishu* if the guests may see the *kogo,* the incense container. Accordingly, the *teishu* places it on the *tatami* in the direction of the guests and then leaves the tearoom, providing time for each guest in turn to inspect and admire it. When all the guests have finished admiring the *kogo,* the main guest will return it to its previous position on the *tatami.* When the *teishu* re-enters, he/she will pick up the *kogo* and then announce that *kaiseki,* a light meal, will now be served.

In a full-length Tea Ceremony, *kaiseki* is customarily served because it is believed that if one has eaten a meal just before the drinking of tea, the taste of the tea will be that much more enhanced. *Kaiseki* is a simple offering consisting of soup, rice, and three side dishes. All courses of the meal are served at the same time on a tray. If a guest cannot finish the meal, he/she will wrap the remainder in a *kaishi,* a paper napkin that he/she has brought along. Even a fish bone will be wrapped up in the *kaishi* and put in one's pocket. All leftovers are taken home by the guests. The *kaiseki* plates are always wiped clean by the guests before passing them back to the *teishu.*

The cleaning of the *kaiseki* plate is considered proper etiquette in the Japanese Tea Ceremony. A plate with food left on it would not look very appealing, so a plate that is being returned to the *teishu* should be clean.

A full-fledged Tea Ceremony consists of three phases: *kaiseki,* the meal, *koicha,* a thick tea, and *usucha,* a thin tea. Guests may leave the tearoom after each phase.

After the light meal, the process of *nakadachi* follows. The guests exit in reverse order of how they entered. In *nakadachi,* one by one, led by the main guest, each guest returns to the *tokonoma* to view the hanging scroll and the flower arrangement. The guests return to the hearth to check if the fire is becoming strong. From there, they return to the garden, where they will pass away the time sitting on the garden bench, exchanging quiet conversation. Many aspects of the Tea Ceremony are performed in reverse order in keeping with its ordered and well-defined nature.

While the guests are conversing in the garden, the *teishu* clears the tearoom and takes down the scroll, replaces the flower arrangement with a hanging flower arrangement, checks the charcoals to make sure the fire is strong, and places incense in it. When these preparations have been made, he/she proceeds to the *dora,* a gong. The gong is hit with certain rhythmic strikes to beckon the guests to re-enter the tearoom. As the *dora* is being struck, the guests respond immediately by crouching to listen attentively to its sounds.

When the final sound of the gong has faded, guests return to the *tsukubai,* the earthenware water basin. Each will perform the cleansing rites again. Then, led by the main guest, one by one the guests will re-enter the tearoom.

This second entering is referred to as the *goziari.* To perform this part of the ceremony, the guests will go first to the alcove and admire the new hanging flower arrangement. Next they go to the fireplace, turn to the shelf, and admire again the *cha-ire,* the tea caddy. They will observe the beautiful *mizusashi,* the water container set on the floor by the shelf.

Before the guests return to their places on the *tatami,* and when the last guest has re-entered the tearoom, the *teishu* will begin the *koicha,* the most formal and honored event in the Tea Ceremony. *Koicha* is a thick tea prepared from *matcha,* powdered *gyokuro* tea leaves, the finest of Japanese teas. During this part of the ceremony, all of the guests will partake in the drinking of *koicha* from the same *chawan,* bowl.

When the *teishu* enters carrying the *chawan,* he/she will bow to all the guests. All the guests will respectfully bow in return. Placed in the bowl is a *chaken,* a tea cloth; a *chasen,* a tea whisk; and a *cha shaku,* a teaspoon for measuring the tea leaves.

The *teishu* kneels down and places the drinking bowl and the tea caddy in front of the *mizusashi,* the water container. He/she then returns to the preparation room and brings back the *kensui,* a waste-water container. In it is placed the *futaoki,* the stand on which the water ladle and the kettle lid will be placed. Laid across the rim of the *kensui* is the *hishaku,* the water ladle. The *teishu* takes the stand out of the *kensui* and sets it and the ladle down on the *tatami* beside the hearth. Having completed this with very precise movements, the *teishu* bows towards the guests and all the guests bow in return. The serving of *koicha* now begins.

The *teishu* organizes the utensils on a serving mat in front of the guests, then removes the *shifuku,* the silk-cloth cover of the tea caddy. He/she cleans the tea utensils with the *fukusa,* a square silk cloth, in front of the guests, even though the utensils have been scrupulously cleaned the morning of the ceremony.

While the *teishu* cleans the tea accoutrements, the guests may listen meditatively to the sounds of the water boiling in the *kama,* the iron kettle. In Japan, the kettle is sometimes referred to as the *Okama,* the "O" prefix signifying its place of honor and respect in the Tea Ceremony.

Following the cleaning of the accoutrements, the *teishu* pours hot water from the kettle into the *chawan*. Then he/she begins the *chasen-toshi*, which is the dipping of the *chasen*, the bamboo whisk, into the hot water to make the bamboo soft. In *chasen-toshi*, the *teishu* turns the whisk around slowly, checking all the tips to make sure they are in perfect shape to make the tea with. Upon approving of the whisk, the *teishu* throws the hot water away into the *kensui*, and dries the bowl with the tea cloth.

In making the *koicha*, the *teishu* takes the *cha shaku*, the teaspoon, with his/her right hand and, picking up the tea caddy with the left hand, dips the spoon into it. Three spoonfuls of the powdered tea per person (fifteen scoops of *matcha* for five guests) are scooped from the tea caddy and put into the *chawan*.

A small amount of hot water is ladled into the cup from the kettle. The *teishu* then takes the bamboo whisk and kneads the powdered tea and water slowly, until the tea is a smooth and creamy consistency. Extra hot water is ladled into the cup to attain the required thickness of the tea.

Once the *koicha* has been made, the *teishu* places the *chawan* and a *dashibukusa*, a silk cloth, in front of the guests. The main guest will come forward and pick up the cup, return with it to his/her place on the *tatami*, and place it and the silk cloth between the next guest in the row and him/herself. The main guest will then bow and all the guests will bow. The main guest will now take the silk cloth and, holding the *chawan*, sip the tea. It is the practice of the *teishu* at this time to ask the main guest how he/she likes the taste of the tea. The main guest will respond, of course, with a compliment such as "the tea has a very nice taste" or "it is very pleasing."

Tea-drinking etiquette dictates that the main guest will sip three and one-half mouthfuls in all, as the tea in this one cup is being shared among all the guests. After sipping, he/she will wipe with the paper napkin the place on the rim that his/her mouth has touched. The main guest now passes the cup and the silk cloth to the next guest, who in turn repeats the procedures and so on.

While the guests are sipping tea, the *teishu* begins the ritual of *nakajumai*, putting the kettle lid back on the kettle and putting away the ladle and the ladle rest. When the *nakajumai* is completed, the *teishu* faces the guests. The main guest may now enquire about the quality of the tea. Questions that could be asked include "what is the name of the tea?" and "where was the tea packed?" In addition, the main guest may ask questions about the scroll, the flower arrangement, or any other subject of interest concerning the present Tea Ceremony.

When the last guest in the line has finished sipping the tea, the *teishu* begins the ritual of *nakajumai-o-toku*, the removal of the kettle's lid. In the meantime, each guest will place the empty cup and the silk cloth in between him/herself and the next guest in line, then bow to that guest. Each will admire the cup by holding it down close to the *tatami* with both hands. When admiring any ceremonial accoutrement, it is important to hold it close to the floor to prevent breakage in case it is dropped accidentally.

When the cup and cloth are returned to the main guest, he/she will inspect them to make sure they have remained in excellent condition after the tea drinking. The *teishu* will then retrieve them and place them in front of him/her. *Koicha* ends with everyone in the tearoom bowing.

The *teishu* now cleans the cup and the tea whisk with water, then performs the *chasen-sugugi,* which is the throwing out of the cleaning water. Next, the *teishu* places the whisk in the cup, cleans the teaspoon with a silk cloth, and arranges the tea caddy and the cup in front of the water jar. The *teishu* then ladles two scoops of water from the water jar into the kettle, in preparation for *usucha,* the final phase of the Tea Ceremony. He/she then places the lids on the kettle and the water jar. Taking the cue from the replacement of the lids, the main guest will ask the *teishu* to see the tea caddy and the teaspoon. The *teishu* will wipe the tea caddy and place it on the *tatami* in front of the main guest. He/she will then place the teaspoon next to the tea caddy and the silk-cloth cover of the tea caddy next to the teaspoon. With the items properly placed, the *teishu* exits the tearoom taking the waste-water container with him/her.

As the *teishu* busies him/herself in the preparation room, the main guest slowly slides forward on the *tatami* towards the tea items, bringing them back and displaying them before him/herself. While this is going on, the *teishu* returns to the tearoom, retrieves the water jar, and again exits to the preparation room. The guests pass each item along to the next, so that each may inspect and admire them. When the last guest has admired the last tea item, all are returned to the *teishu.* The *teishu* inspects the accoutrements and then returns them to their previous places in reverse order.

The *teishu* answers questions at this time about the items. Lastly, the *teishu* takes the tea equipment and leaves the room. All throughout the ceremony, the tea items are returned to the preparation room in reverse order of how they were originally brought into the tearoom. Each time the *teishu* exits the tearoom, he/she bows to the guests and all the guests respectfully bow in return.

Finally, the *Gozumi,* the Second Charcoal Ceremony, begins. The fire by now has burned down, so the *teishu* enters the tearoom with the *sumitori,* the charcoal basket. He/she adds and rearranges the charcoals in the fire, places incense in it again, and adds cold water to the kettle. While waiting for the fire to build up, the guests and *teishu* exchange conversation in a relaxed manner. When the water in the kettle starts to boil, the *teishu* will announce the *usucha*.

The *teishu* washes each cup with hot water and makes cups of tea for each guest, one by one. *Usucha* is whisked faster in comparison to *koicha*. *Usucha* is made with tea leaves instead of powder and has a light froth when served.

Guests snack on desserts while the tea is being made. *Okashi,* a sweet dessert usually made from azuki-bean paste, may be served. The type of sweets served will depend on the month and the season in which the Tea Ceremony is taking place. For example, in February, a *teishu* would serve *umegoromo* (plum robe) sweets. Plum trees blossom in February in Japan, so desserts are created in a plum-blossom design at this time. Desserts are often also molded into figures, such as birds or cherries, reflecting the current season.

After *usucha,* the main guest thanks the *teishu* for the ceremony. Following this lead, all the other guests thank the host/ess. The *teishu* in turn thanks each guest for coming. Lastly, all the guests thank each other and leave.

Tea caddy (cha-ire), *teaspoon* (cha shaku), *tea bowl* (chawan), *and water ladle* (hishaku).

The day after the ceremony, the guests will perform *zenrei,* which is visiting the *teishu* again for a quick and quiet moment to express their gratitude for a fine ceremony well performed.

Note: The preceding Japanese Tea Ceremony description is based on the principles of the *Omete Senke* School of Tea in Japan.

Japanese Tea Ceremony Terms

The Japanese have a delightful vocabulary describing the Tea Ceremony:

cha—tea

chabana—flower arrangement for a tea gathering

cha-ire—tea caddy, container for *koicha,* a thick tea

chaken—tea cloth

chasen—bamboo tea whisk

chasen-sugugi—process of throwing away the waste water, used to clean tea accoutrements during the Tea Ceremony

chasen-toshi—process of dipping the bamboo whisk into hot water to soften the bamboo

cha shaku—teaspoon/tea scoop; measure for tea

chashitsu—tearoom, which is an enclosure partitioned off in a house, not an individual structure or teahouse

chawan—the cup for drinking *koicha*

dashibukusa—silk cloth, thicker than a *fukusa,* used during the formal *koicha* phase of the ceremony to hold the chawan

dora—gong sounded by the *teishu* signalling the guests to return to the tearoom

fukusa—square piece of silk cloth, which each guest brings

furo—hibachi-type hearth used in the Tea Ceremony from May 1 to October 31

futaoki—stand on which are set the kettle lid and the water ladle

goziari—process of the guests entering the tearoom for a second time

Gozumi—Second Charcoal Ceremony

hanto—helper chosen to aid the *teishu*

higashi—dry sweets

hishaku—water ladle

kaiseki—light meal

kaishi—small, white paper napkin, which each guest brings

kakemono—calligraphic scroll painting that states the reason why the Tea Ceremony is taking place *kama*—iron kettle, also referred to as the *Okama,* the initial "O" signifying the kettle's place of honor and respect in the Japanese Tea Ceremony

kensui—waste-water container

ko—incense

kogo—incense container

koicha—thick tea, made with *matcha*

koshikake—garden bench with cushions on it

kyaku—guest or guests invited to the Tea Ceremony

matcha—powdered tea used to make *koicha*; *matcha* is made from the finest *gyokuro* tea leaves

mizusashi—ceramic water jar

mizuya—preparation room, where the tea equipment is washed and stored

nakadachi—the process of guests exiting the tearoom

nakajumai—procedure of putting the lid on the kettle and of putting away the ladle and ladle rest

nakajumai-o-toku—procedure of removing the kettle's lid and taking out again the ladle and ladle rest

nijiriguchi—three-foot-high sliding door going from the outside of the house to the tearoom

niwa—garden

Ocha—tea is often referred to by the Japanese as *Ocha* (see *cha*), signifying the honor and respect accorded to tea in Japan

Ochaji—complete formal Tea Ceremony with a light meal

okashi—sweet dessert usually made from azuki-bean paste

ro—fire hearth used in the wintertime ceremonies, November 1 to April 30

roji—direct translation is "dewy path," referring to the pathway through the garden

shifuku—silk-cloth cover of the *cha-ire,* the tea caddy

shokyaku—main guest chosen to represent all of the guests at the Tea Ceremony

shotaijo—invitations sent to the guests

Shozumi—First Charcoal Ceremony

sumi—charcoals for the fire

sumi-temai—Charcoal Ceremony (see *Shozumi* and *Gozumi*)

sumitori—charcoal basket

tatami—rice straw mats on the floor; one *tatami* (three feet by six feet) is considered the proper size for one person (in Japan, the *tatami* is an architectural measuring unit)

teishu—host/ess of the Tea Ceremony

tokonoma—alcove where the scroll and the flower arrangement are placed; the most honored place in a tearoom

tsukubai—earthenware water basin placed in the garden; used for purification rites

umegoromo—translates to "plum robe"; sweets/dessert

usucha—thin tea

yoritsuki—waiting room or portico specifically established for the guests to assemble at the beginning of the Tea Ceremony

yu—heated water

zenrei—thanking the *teishu* for the invitation to the *Ochaji*

From the Tea Estate to You

To many tea drinkers, the word "tea" means green tea (coming from China and Japan), or black tea (from Africa, India, and Sri Lanka). Teas are botanically classified as *Camellia sinensis,* which are teas from China, and *Camellia assamica,* which are teas that originated from plants in the Assam region of northern India. Occasionally, there is a third classification, *Camellia japonica,* which is tea grown in Japan. All tea, however, originated from the *Camellia sinensis* plant.

There is a myth that there is a special type of tea plant that produces green leaves and another type that produces black leaves. In fact, the difference in color that we observe in the tea leaf as it goes into the teapot is dependent on manufacturing processes. A black tea leaf is produced when a green tea leaf goes through a fermentation and oxidation process. All tea originates from a green-leafed plant.

In the Beginning . . .

Tea cultivation and tea manufacturing methods in the major tea estate countries have remained largely unchanged for generations. The tea plant begins its life as a tea seed or cutting planted in a nursery and grown there until the plant is about fifteen months old. It is then planted on the estate, where it will continue its growth for at least three more years, until it is mature enough to be plucked.

Tea plants are grown at various elevations, from sea level to hilly and mountainous areas. A tea plant may take several more years to reach its maturity at high elevations than at low ones. As a general rule, the higher the elevation a tea plant is grown on, the better the quality of the tea. Most of the world's teas are grown in humid mountainous areas on either side of the equator.

About three thousand tea plants, spaced three to four feet apart, decorate each acre of a tea estate. Tea estates generally range in size from 300 to 3,000 acres.

Normally maintained as a bush of three to four feet in height (a good height for picking), a tea plant, if left unpruned, would grow to become a tree of thirty or more feet in height. In some tea-growing areas where conditions permit, the plants

61

are plucked from every seven to fifteen days. In other tea-growing areas of the world such as China, India, and Japan, the tea harvesting is seasonal.

From its first plucking, a single tea plant will probably continue to be harvested for the next half-century or more. With the appearance of the "first flush" (the first two leaves and a flower bud), the tea plant will be plucked by dedicated tea estate laborers, who work the estate by going from plant to plant pinching off the top two leaves and flowering bud. An experienced worker can pick 36 kg. (79.2 lb.) of top-leaf growth and leaf buds in a day.

When the tea baskets are full, they are left along the roadside where another group of workers separates out any stems or shoots from the leaves and buds.

A Sri Lankan tea picker.

THE TEA BOOK

Baskets of the separated tea materials are then transported to the tea estate factory by any means of transportation available on the estate, ranging from trucks to wagons driven by oxen.

At the Factory

The tea factory is the most significant-looking building on the tea estate. Always several stories high, the factory has different tea-related activities on each story.

Once at the factory, the tea leaves are spaced out evenly on racks, so they may begin to lose some of their moisture and wither. This withering process makes the tea leaves soft and pliable. Withering takes between eighteen and twenty-four hours.

When the tea leaves reach their optimum pliable state, they are rolled into the characteristic twists and curls that we tea drinkers are so familiar with. Nowadays, rolling machines roll the tea leaves. But for centuries (and still in some places in China and Japan), the tea leaves were hand-rolled. The rolling of the leaves is an essential part of manufacturing tea. It breaks down the leaf cells and releases the tea leaves' natural juices.

After the rolling, the tea leaves are put through a process of fermentation. This

Withering racks.

A rolling machine.

In the fermentation room, the tea leaves are fermented (oxidized) until they reach a copper color. This process is used in making black tea.

process makes the unique difference between a green tea leaf and a black tea leaf. To make green tea, the leaves are fired right after picking. Firing stops fermentation and extracts further moisture from the leaf. A green leaf has about 77 percent moisture; a fired leaf between 4 and 6 percent. The firing is done in ovens in which the heat ranges from 120 degrees F in the early stages to 200 degrees F in the final stage. Firing takes about twenty minutes.

However, to make black tea, the green leaves are placed for three hours on a cement slab in a cool, humid room, referred to as the "fermentation room." This natural process of fermentation allows the leaves to absorb oxygen. When the leaves are oxidized, they turn a bright copper color. The black tea smell will be present. One hundred kg. (220 lb.) of green leaves makes about 20 kg. (44 lb.) of black tea.

Finally, the fermented copper-colored leaves are layered on racks in an iron chamber referred to as the "hot room." Hot dry air is continuously forced into the chamber, further drying the leaves until the oxidation has stopped. Black tea will now preserve well until it is exported from the tea estate to the millions of teapots around the world.

The leaves are dried to stop the fermentation, ending up dark colored or black.

Tea Grading

Over the years the method of tea-leaf grading has changed very little. Such grading gives a complete story about the tea by analyzing the characteristics of the leaves, which ultimately leads to what the tea infusion in the teacup will taste like.

The grading begins by labelling the tea leaves according to the country and estate where they were grown. The labelling automatically tells a tea-grading expert much about the climate and soil conditions, which will affect the overall quality of the tea.

In Sri Lanka, teas may also be classified according to the elevation at which they are grown. Sri Lankans refer to teas as being high grown (over 4,000 feet), medium grown (1,600-4,000 feet), or low grown (below 1,600 feet). Generally speaking, the higher the elevation, the more delicate the tea. Low-grown teas are usually stronger and plainer tasting.

WHOLE LEAVES

After the variety of tea leaves and the geographic location are identified, teas are further classified according to whether they are whole or broken into smaller-sized pieces.

Whole tea leaves and tea leaf pieces are put through various sorting machines comprising sieves with different-sized meshes. The leaves are labelled by grade, according to the size of the openings in the mesh that they have fallen through. In grading, all of the above-ground parts of the tea plant—the leaves, the stems, and the twigs—will be identified by grade.

The highest of the graded teas are Flowering Orange Pekoe and Orange Pekoe. The term *Pekoe* originated from the Chinese word *Pek-ho,* meaning "white hairs." It describes the tiny white hairs that grow on the tips of tea leaves.

Flowering Orange Pekoe (F.O.P.): the first two leaves and leaf bud of the first growth in a season. Tea estate workers walk along from plant to plant pinching off these first growths. Stems and twigs are removed. The leaves and bud will pass through a specific-sized mesh sieve. The bud is not a flower bud but the budding growth of a tea leaf, or "tip."

Pekoe (P.): a small, well-twisted, rolled leaf with a thin appearance and a good-colored liquor.

Orange Pekoe (O.P.): a certain-sized mesh is used to shake through the

The leaves are sorted into chests for export.

small young leaves. Those that pass through the mesh are graded Orange Pekoe. The leaves are tightly twisted with a wiry appearance and usually contain tip. The *Orange* in the name has nothing to do with the grade, but is a marketing term that probably originated with the House of Orange, a princely dynasty of the Netherlands.

Pekoe Souchong (P.S.): the first growth leaves of the *Souchong* variety of tea plant, passed through a certain-sized mesh. Those that pass through a pekoe-sized mesh are called *Pekoe Souchong*. Souchong leaves are crisper and coarser than other grades. They produce a paler liquor. *Souchong* derives its name from the Chinese word *siao-chung,* meaning "larger sort," describing the long and slender leaves.

The Souchong is of a larger and coarser grade than the Flowering Orange Pekoe, Pekoe, and Orange Pekoe grades.

BROKEN LEAVES

Broken Pekoe (B.P.): those leaves that do not pass through the pekoe-sized meshes. Broken tea leaves are used in tea bags because they infuse faster than larger whole leaves. This grade usually contains tip.

Broken Orange Pekoe (B.O.P.): smaller than the whole-leaf grades, usually contains tip, and produces a good-bodied cup.

Broken Souchong (B.S.): coarser than Broken Pekoe; paler in the cup than other broken-leaf grades.

Fannings (F.): very small bits of tea stems and leaves, which fall through the smallest grade of mesh sieves. Originally, these extrafine pieces were separated by a hot-air, fanning process. Nowadays they are mechanically separated.

Dust (D): the smallest pieces of tea grade that have fallen away or have been separated from the larger tea-leaf pieces. Dust pieces are smaller than fannings, and are used in blends for tea bags for quick infusions. As a rule, the smaller the grade, the quicker and darker the infusion.

Note: These are the tea grades for Sri Lanka. There is also a Bohea grade. Tea grading varies somewhat in China, India, and Indonesia.

Tea Tasting

When the tea lover goes to a specialty store or commercial grocery outlet to purchase a favorite blend of tea leaves, it is expected that, each time, this blend will taste the same. It is the responsibility of tea tasters to maintain this consistency among teas and tea blends. With astonishing ability, an expert or Master Taster can usually identify about 1,500 varieties of tea and the characteristics common to each.

An experienced taster can tell an entire story about a tea from sampling an infusion. To the taster, the infusion illuminates which geographical area the tea comes from, how long the tea will keep, and what characteristics the tea will have. Each variety has a distinct color and taste. The flavor in tea is considered by connoisseurs to be a combination of aroma, body, and pungency. Teas have essential oils that give them their aroma and flavor.

A Master Taster.

69

Tea tasting has employed the same methods since the early 1800s. They vary little from country to country and from estate to estate. First, the taster evaluates the tea leaves for their dryness, crispness, and the type of roll or twist they have. Next, the evenness or consistency in appearance of all the leaves together is graded, as well as if there are any twigs or stems present in the grade. The complexion or greyness of the batch is then judged.

Tea tasting has a unique vocabulary of its own. Following is a list of some of the terms used by tea tasters to judge the appearance of the tea leaves:

Gold Tip or Tippy: when the young tea leaves are rolled, juices squeeze out and stain the white hairs on the underside, giving the leaves a golden color. Gold Tip or tippy tea leaves are considered to be of good quality. Hand-rolled tea leaves have a better tip than machine-rolled ones.

Silver Tip: overwithered tea leaves, resulting in grey tips on the leaves.

Bold: the tea-leaf pieces are too big for the grade being considered by the tasters.

Even: the leaf grade is consistent; denotes the tea-leaf pieces are roughly the same size.

Uneven: the tea leaves are inconsistent in size, usually indicating a poor sorting of the leaves.

Clean: the leaves are free from dust and fiber.

Tea tasters also judge the body and the color of a brewed tea. When tea is cooled, there is a resulting body or thickness to it, caused by the polyphenol compounds and essential oils in the tea. Body refers to the "feeling of weight" the liquor has in the mouth and on the tongue. The way a tea infusion "creams down" determines the body of the tea. A very dilute infusion indicates poor tea leaves and an undesirable tea.

The color of the tea infusion is then observed. Color will vary depending on the tea variety and location of cultivation:

Bright: the infusion is a bright color, usually indicating an "alive" tea.

Dull: the infusion looks muddy, opposite of bright; this is usually indicative of a poorly manufactured tea or of inferior-quality tea leaves.

Copper: denotes a good-quality tea.

Green: indicates that black tea leaves have not been fermented enough or have been under-rolled.

Orange: a good color; will be amber when milk is added.

Light: a poor-bodied tea, resulting from inferior leaves.

Heavy: strong-colored tea liquor (refers to black teas), thick, lacks briskness.

The aroma that the tea leaves give off comes across in the tea infusion. This fragrance is also referred to as the "nose" of the tea:

Bouquet: the complete aroma of the tea.

Flowery: the fragrant aroma of some of the best or finest teas.

Burnt: smells of burnt material; the firing temperature of the tea leaves was probably too high.

Coarse: infusion is devoid of aroma; this denotes coarse leaves.

Tainted: tea has a foreign smell, indicating that the tea leaves may have come into contact with foreign agents such as onions; could also denote a bacterial infection or mold. Often described as having "gone off."

Tasters evaluate the tea according to taste. The following excerpt is from a brochure titled "Talented Tasters" sent to the author from Lyons Tetley Ltd.

> Tea for tasting is brewed in a very particular way, unchanged for over a hundred years. . . . The water is boiled on gas rings in specially made wide-bottom copper kettles, and it must be precisely at boiling point when it is poured over the leaves. For sampling purposes, exactly 6.5 grammes [.23 oz.] of tea—the equivalent of two old six penny pieces—is weighed into a special white china mug, with a lid.
>
> The liquor is made at three times the normal strength and the tea is brewed for exactly six minutes. When the liquor is poured out, the mug is turned upside down and the leaves are left on the lid for the taster to see. Tetley's tasters are able to tell from these leaves or infusion what the characteristics of that tea should be and how well it will keep.
>
> The tea is tasted with milk because that is how most people in Britain drink it. It is sucked sharply from a spoon onto the back of the palate, rolled around the mouth to pick up such characteristics as thickness and degree and type of flavour, before being deposited into a spittoon.

Dried tea leaves pick up the taste and smell of foreign agents very easily. Well-trained tasters can taste in the infusion any characteristic that is alien to the tea leaves. Some terms used to describe unacceptable infusions are:

Fruity: usually indicative of a bacterial infection. Not to be confused with the fruity character of Oolong teas.

Sweaty: tastes the way sweat smells; the tea leaves have been overfermented or a bacterial infection is present.

Burnt: tastes burnt; the tea leaves have been overfired or fired on too high a temperature.

Tea tasters watch the way the leaves unroll in the boiling water. This unrolling is referred to as the "agony of tea leaves." Leaves that are flat or have a loose roll will infuse faster in the water. Leaves that have a tighter roll or are well twisted will infuse slower, taking a longer time to emit their essences.

The Tea-Growing Countries

There are thousands of tea estates in the world in over thirty-five countries. The sheer number of estates makes it impossible to list them all. Briefly then, following are the countries in which tea is grown throughout the world.

Africa: Cameroon, Kenya (formerly British East Africa), Malagasy Republic (formerly Madagascar), Malawi (formerly Nyasaland), Mauritius, Mozambique, Rwanda, Seychelles, South Africa, Tanzania (formerly Tanganyika and Zanzibar), Uganda, Zaire (formerly Congo Free State, Belgian Congo, Democratic Republic of Congo), Zambia (formerly Northern Rhodesia), Zimbabwe (formerly Southern Rhodesia)

Central Asia: Bangladesh (formerly East Pakistan), Commonwealth of Independent States (formerly the U.S.S.R.), India, Iran, Sri Lanka (formerly Ceylon), Turkey

Far East: China, Indonesia (Java, Sumatra), Japan, Kampuchea (Cambodia), Malaysia, Myanmar (formerly Burma), Papua New Guinea (formerly British Guinea), Taiwan (formerly Formosa), Thailand, Vietnam

South America: Argentina, Brazil, Ecuador, Peru

Tea Varieties and Grades from Around the World

BANGLADESH

Black teas from the Sylhet District (part of the Surma Valley) are manufactured here. These teas are referred to as *Sylhets* or *Chittagongs,* the latter being named after the port of Chittagong.

The Tea-Growing Countries

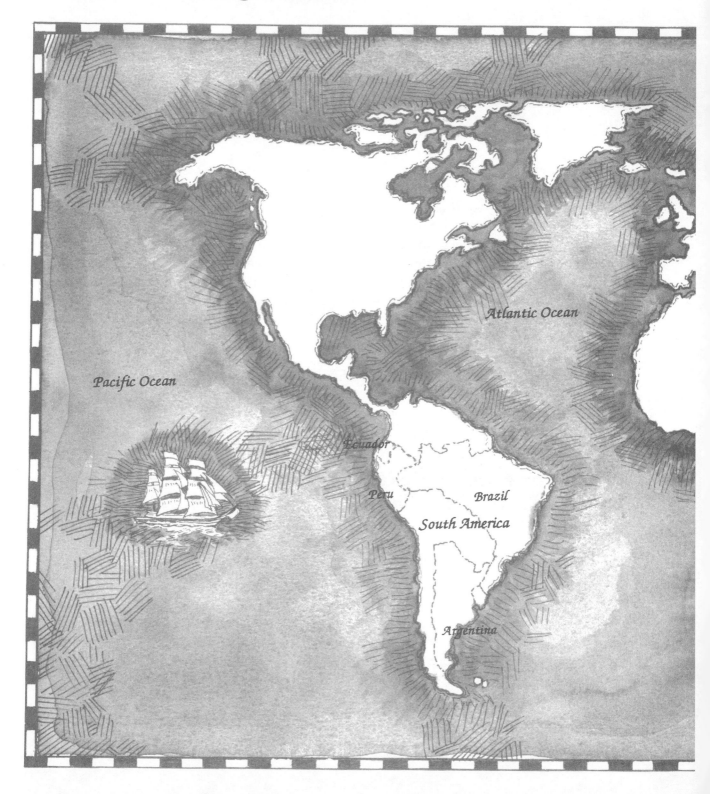

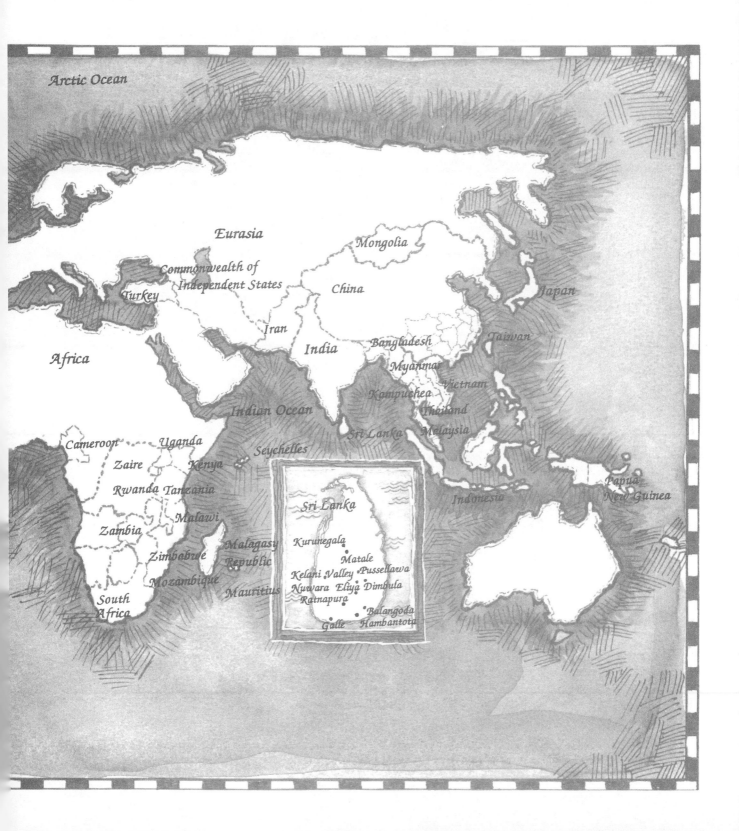

HONG CHA (RED TEAS)

In China, black teas are referred to as "red teas." It is the Western world that refers to the fermented tea as "black tea."

Bohea: from the Bohea area, Fukien province of China. Documented as one of the first cultivated varieties of the *Camellia sinensis.* These days, bohea is lightly fermented. Its brew is a deep yellow color.

Congous: derived from the word *koong-fu,* meaning "the laborious sort." The manufacturing process is longer than for most tea leaves. Nowadays, *congous* is a term applied to all red teas from China. Teas are divided into "North China Congous" and "South China Congous." Gradings are similar to those in India and Sri Lanka.

Souchong/Lapsang Souchong: long, slender leaves that are crisper than other tea-leaf varieties. The tea is amber colored and slightly acidic with a faint smoky or tarry taste, which is what makes it so appealing to many of its connoisseurs.

LIU CHA (GREEN TEAS)

The green teas of China are also referred to as the *Country Greens.* China produces many grades of green teas. Here are a few, classified according to age and leaf style.

Gunpowder: a well-known tea, so named because the tea leaf is only twice the size of a medium-sized piece of gunpowder. The unfermented young leaves unroll when steeped, producing a light-bodied tea.

Imperial: looser-rolled balls of tea, left over from Gunpowder tea; usually older leaves.

Singlo and Twankay: an open-leaf grade of older-growth leaves, which yield an inferior tea.

Young Hyson: small to medium-size leaves that are long, narrow, and twisted (or similar in appearance to Gunpowder).

Hyson: looser-twisted leaves compared to the Young Hyson; the leaves are old growth and produce an inferior tea. Hyson is often mixed with jasmine petals to produce jasmine tea. This variety is named after Mr. Hyson, an East Indian merchant.

Hyson Skin: older leaves producing an inferior tea.

Sowmee: grade of poorer-quality tea; pieces are small, but larger than fannings.

Fannings: the second-smallest tea grade.
Dust: the leftovers.

OTHER CHINESE TEA VARIETIES AND GRADES

Teas are often named for the geographical area from which they came. For example, teas from Guangdong province may be referred to as *Guangdongs.* Teas are sometimes named for the shipping center they are exported from. The main tea shipping centers in China are Canton (now called Guangzhou), Foochow, and Shanghai, so teas may be loosely referred to as "Cantons," "Foochows," or "Shanghais."

Following are some of the areas of China that grow tea and the varieties grown there.

Anhwei: Moyunes, Tienkaid (green teas), Keemuns (red teas)

Chekiang: Hoochows, Pingsueys (green teas)

Fukien: Lapsang Souchong, Padres, Paklings, Paklums, Panyongs, Chingwos, Ti-Kuan-Yin (red teas). Fukien teas are sold through the Foochow market. Teas sold through this market are often referred to as "Foochow Teas."

Guangdong: teas from this area are known as Cantons and Guangdongs

Hunan: Ichangs, Keemuns, Ningchows, Onfars (red teas)

Hupeh: Keemuns, Ningchows, Oonams (red teas), Pingsueys (green teas)

Kiangsi: Ningchows (red teas)

Kiangsu: Keemuns, Ningchows (red teas)

Teas are also grown in Guizhou, Szechuan, and Yunnan, the southwest provinces.

INDIA

Grades of green teas in India are similar to those of China. Gradings are labelled *Fine Young Hyson, Young Hyson, Hyson No. 1, Twankay, Sowmee, Fannings,* and *Dust.*

Eighty percent of India's teas are processed into black tea. Most of India's teas are used in blends except for the highest quality Assams and some Darjeelings. The leaf gradings for black teas are similar to those in Sri Lanka, with the exception that altitude is not important in grade labelling (see "Tea Grading").

NORTHERN INDIA

Varieties grown in northern India include:

Kangra
Mandi
Dehra Dun

Northeast India grows the finest teas in the world. Teas are grown in the Assam Valley, which is subdivided into the Brahmaputra Valley and the Surma Valley. Collectively, teas from these areas are known as Assams:

Brahmaputra Valley: part of the Assam Valley
Lakhimpur District: these teas are among the finest of the Assams, grown around Dum Duma
Sibsagar District: teas known as Sibsagars
Darrang District: teas known as Darrangs
Nowgong District: teas known as Nowgongs
Surma Valley: part of the Assam Valley
Cachar District: teas known as Cachars

The following varieties are also found in northeast India:

Darjeeling: grown in the foothills of the Himalayas
Terai: teas known as Terais
Dooars: teas known as Dooars
Ranchi

SOUTHERN INDIA

Areas in southern India where tea is grown include the following.

Karnataka District
Tamil Nadu District: Nilgiris in the Blue Mountains, one of the first areas of India where the British were successful in cultivating tea; Coimbatore
Kerala District (formerly Travancore): Kanan Devan District, Mundakayam

INDONESIA

Indonesian tea grades are much the same as those in Sri Lanka (see "Tea Grading") except that Indonesia has two different categories of Broken Pekoes: a Broken

Tea Grade and a Bohea Grade. Teas are produced in Java and Sumatra and are known by the islands from which they come.

JAPAN

The Japanese prefer to classify their green teas according to their use.

Bancha: the three-year-old growth of twigs and leaves from a variety of tea bushes or the leaves that are picked at the end of the season. Bancha is the most commonly used tea in the households of Japan.

Sencha: the special tea that the Japanese people serve their guests. Considered a medium-grade tea, sencha is the younger-growth leaves of the tea plant. The tea preparation does not contain stems or twigs.

Gyokuro: the highest-quality sencha, the first growth ("the first flush") of the tea bush. This tea is unique because the bushes are planted in shaded areas, causing the leaves to become a purple-green or blue-green color. During the manufacturing process, the leaves are specially rolled by hand. Gyokuro, with its light sweetness and deep flavor, is considered the finest tea in Japan. The Japanese word *gyokuro* means "Pearl Dew," a name that has become commercially synonymous with the tea itself. The tea is also referred to as "Jewel Dew."

Tencha: the green tea used primarily for the Japanese Tea Ceremony. It is a blend of Uji and Nagoya gyokuro leaves. The main distinction of tencha is its color. Blue-green leaves are used to make usucha, a thin tea; and purple and dark green leaves are used to make koicha, a thick tea.

Classification may also be done according to leaf-style preparation and manufacturing process. Extra firing of the leaves is done to ensure that they are moisture free.

Pan-fired: small leaves rubbed in hot metal pans. The leaves may be straight or lightly curled. The process produces polished-looking leaves.

Guri: very curly tea leaves that are pan-fired.

Basket-fired: long, thin, young tea leaves that are twisted and fired in baskets. Basket-fired leaves are longer than pan-fired.

Natural leaf: other tea leaves fired in hot iron pans or baskets (e.g., sencha).

Gradings of sencha are labelled Extra Choicest, Choicest, Choice, Finest, Fine, Good Medium, Good Common, Nibs, Fannings, and Dust.

TAIWAN (FORMERLY FORMOSA)

Formosa Oolong: a semifermented tea, yielding a gold-colored tea with a slight fruity taste. To produce Formosa Oolong, the leaves undergo a partial withering process. Immediately afterwards the leaves are dried, rolled, and fired. This tea is gaining in popularity on the world market. The tea is grown on family farms in Taiwan. The name *Oolong* was originally *ou-long* or *wu lung* and means "black dragon."

Gradings are similar to those used by the Japanese. Categories qualifying the Oolongs, for example, are Choice, Finest to Choice, Finest, Fine to Finest, Fine Up, Fine, On Fine, Superior to Fine, Superior Up, Fully Superior, Superior, On Superior, Good to Superior, Good Up, Fully Good, Good, On Good, Standard.

Taiwan produces *Pouchongs,* which are tea leaves that are fermented for a shorter period of time than Oolong leaves. They are scented with flower blossoms (e.g., gardenia, jasmine, lichee).

Tea Brewing Methods

Steeping or Infusion

According to the English, "only in England can a perfect cup of tea be made." The infusion method of making tea is as popular today as it has ever been. Following are the instructions for making what is referred to as "the perfect cup of tea":

Wash the teapot well in sudsy water. Polyphenols can collect in the teapot and if they are left there they will go rancid and produce a bitter-tasting tea in the pot.

Warm the teapot by swishing it with boiling water. A warmed teapot will help keep the tea warm. Dry the teapot before pouring in the tea water.

Bring fresh water to a boil in a stainless-steel, nonreactive pot. Remove the pot from the heat as soon as the water starts to roll. Do not use water that has been previously boiled.

Put 1 tsp. of quality-grade tea leaves per 6 oz. of boiling water into the teapot. Bring the teapot to the water pot, to minimize loss of heat, and pour the boiling water over the tea leaves. (Always place tea leaves in the teapot before pouring in boiling

A lotus-shaped Yi-Hsing teapot.

water. Never sprinkle the tea leaves over the water.) Cover the teapot with its lid and steep the tea for a prescribed 3-5 minutes. Serve the tea immediately after it has been steeped. In England it is considered proper etiquette to make the tea in the pot first, before transferring it to cups. Tea made in a cup is taboo.

Many people follow a "five minute" steeping rule for making tea. During this time, the rolled leaves unfold and release their properties. At around the five-minute mark there is a balance of the caffeine and the polyphenols released into the hot water. The resulting tea boasts a good flavor, without an acidic taste.

Note: Remove the tea leaves from the pot, if all the tea is not being drunk right away. Oversteeping or "stewing" tea draws out more polyphenols from the leaves, giving a bitter taste. Also, do not squeeze or press the wet tea leaves to extract flavor or moisture. Excess and harsher-tasting polyphenols will be released into the brew.

Also note that steeping the tea leaves for a longer period of time will not compensate for using a smaller quantity of leaves or for using an inferior grade of tea.

Most tea companies provide instructions on their packaging for infusing their tea. Infusion time depends on the tea variety, the size of the leaves or blend, the parts of the plant used, and the manufacturing process.

To remove leaves from the pot, strain the tea into another pot or use a teapot with a removable strainer basket. Wire-mesh tea balls are also useful for making tea in a pot.

TEA WATER

Tea is best made with water at boiling-point temperature, or "water just off the boil." The reason for this approach is that many tea leaves infuse best at this water temperature (200-205 degrees F). Aerated water also produces a better-tasting tea. The air in water "just off the boil" helps to distribute the tea leaves in the pot, so that the hot water can have the maximum infusing effect over the mass surface of the leaves. Water that has been boiled for too long or is de-aerated brews a flat tea.

In A.D. 780, Lu Yu revealed his own brewing technique. His instructions were as follows: "Wait until the water boils. When there are bubbles that resemble crystal beads rolling in a fountain, it is time to pour water over the leaves."

When using soft water for tea, choose leaves with a looser twist, as they emit their flavor more easily. When using hard water, choose leaves with a tighter roll or curl because they release their essences slower. Finally, use clean, cold tap water for your tea water. The less chemically fluoride-treated the water is, the better. Some people now prefer to use charcoal-filtered water for brewing tea. The filters reduce the water's copper and lead content. They also reduce the chlorine taste.

Decoction

Parts of tea plants (leaves, stems) are boiled to extract their properties. The resulting liquid is called a decoction. Originally tea was made by the decoction method. In some countries such as India and Libya, tea is still made by boiling the tea leaves in water.

Tea Essence

Russian-style tea is made with a tea essence. A strong tea essence can be made by infusing 1 tsp. of tea leaves in ½ cup of boiling water. The leaves are infused in the water for a long period of time (10 minutes or longer) over low heat, producing a bitter-tasting essence. The resulting strong essence is then used in small amounts to mix with boiling water in the teacups. Each tea drinker can make tea to his or her own preferred strength.

To make tea: Fill each teacup one-quarter to one-third full with tea essence. Then fill up the rest of each cup with boiling water. (For other tea essence recipes, see "Traditional Tea Recipes"—Commonwealth of Independent States, Iran, Poland, and Turkey.)

Contemporary Methods

Contemporary tea-making methods all involve infusion. To begin, water is boiled in a teakettle rather than in an open pot. A teakettle is a metal pot with a handle, lid, and spout. It may be stove-top heated or electrically heated. Electric kettles have a self-contained heating element on the base. Water is poured into the kettle and heated to boiling point (steam escaping through the spout makes the kettle whistle, announcing the readiness of the water). The boiling water is then poured into a teapot or teacups in which tea leaves have been placed.

TEAPOT AND CUP STRAINER

One contemporary infusion method involves pouring boiling water into a teapot containing loose leaves (see "Steeping" above for detailed instructions), steeping the tea, and then pouring the brew over a cup strainer. This is usually metal meshed and colander shaped. Its purpose is to separate the tea leaves from the liquid. The round metal-framed strainer rests over the mouth of the teacup, catching the loose leaves as the brew is poured from the teapot. This allows the server to tip the teapot to its maximum.

Apart from the usual aluminum mesh strainers, decoratively designed silver-plated and stainless-steel cup strainers are also available. Basket-shaped teapot strainers can also be purchased. They can simply be lifted out of the pots once the leaves are steeped.

IN-CUP FILTER

It is possible to go from the teakettle straight to the cup, eliminating the need for a teapot. There is a filter that can rest inside a teacup. Loose tea is put into the filter and boiling water is poured through it and into the cup. A lid is placed over the cup and the tea leaves are steeped right in the cup. After the tea leaves are infused, the filter containing them is removed.

Often an in-cup filter is designed specifically to fit the cup it is purchased with. *Note:* For in-cup filters, use 1 tsp. tea leaves per 6 oz. boiling water.

TEA BALL/TEA EGG

A tea ball (often referred to as a *tea egg*) is a perforated-metal, ball-shaped container in which tea leaves are placed. The ball is immersed in a teacup of boiling water, so the properties of the tea leaves can seep out through the small perforations without any leaves escaping into the liquid. If desired, place a lid or a saucer over the teacup when the tea is steeping. Larger tea balls can be used to infuse tea leaves in a teapot.

When using a tea ball, fill it to one-half full with the tea leaves, leaving enough room in it for the leaves to expand. Remove the ball from the cup or pot when the desired amount of infusion has been achieved, so that further infusion will not take place.

A small chain with a hook on the end of it is attached to each tea ball. The tea drinker attaches the hook to the rim of the pot or cup, allowing the tea ball to be lifted out easily after the infusion. Decorative stop bowls are available to hold dripping tea balls that have just been removed from water.

Note: The advantage of using the tea ball or the in-cup filter is that any blend of loose tea can be selected for use. Also, tea drinkers can create their own blends to suit their taste by combining herbs and spices with the loose tea. When making larger pots of tea, two or more tea balls may be immersed in the hot water, allowing the herbs, spices, and tea leaves to be infused at the same time. It should be noted, however, that perforated tea balls do not make as good infusers as metal mesh ones because the essences are not emitted into the water as easily.

TEA PRESS POT/GERMAN BODUM OR FRENCH PRESS POT (PLUNGER POT METHOD)

The tea press pot is cylindrical in shape and usually made of glass. The pot has a plunging apparatus to force the tea leaves to the bottom once the tea is steeped. The plunger is made of a metal filter or sieve attached to a spoke coming from the lid. It acts as a strainer, allowing the tea liquid to stay on top while settling the leaves on the bottom.

Tea ball in a stop bowl.

Tea press pots can have the disadvantage of producing a bitter-tasting tea because the leaves are pressed by the plunger. This pressing emits harsher-tasting elements into the water. When buying a press pot, purchase one that has the plunger extended through the lid and separate in function from it. When the tea is steeped, press the plunger to the top layer of expanded tea leaves. It is helpful to use broken-grade teas in press pots, as these grades rarely ever expand beyond the vacuum created for them at the bottom of the pot. With "brokens," the plunger can usually be pushed downwards fully.

Recently tea cozies have been designed to fit this contemporary-shaped pot. Because press pots are made of glass, they tend to cool off quicker than their porcelain or earthenware counterparts. Also, the glassware cylinder can break. Tea cozies (padded cloth covers) prolong the warmth of the tea and protect the pot.

Replacement cylinders are readily available from the manufacturer and usually from the outlet where the pot was purchased.

To make tea: Place 1 tsp. tea leaves per 6 oz. hot water in the bottom of the pot. Add boiling water. Let the tea steep for 3-5 minutes. Take the plunger lid and place it in the pot. Plunge the pot filter downwards until it presses all the tea leaves down to the bottom of the pot. Pour tea into cups.

TEA BAG

The tea bag infusion is the most popular method of making tea in the Western hemisphere. The tea bag itself is made of specially treated, perforated paper, processed from the stems of Manila hemp. The fiber and design of the bag is well suited to different blends of "broken" tea leaves. The paper prevents the release of tea particles into the water.

Tea bags usually contain the lower grades of tea (fannings and dust) and cut-and-torn "broken" leaves of better grades. Modern tea-picking machines used in some parts of the world are not capable of only removing the top two leaves and the bud of the tea plants. Thus, in their grabbing movements, they snap off other parts of the plant, such as twigs and stems, all of which may end up in the tea bag. This process of tea picking is called *C.T.C. (Cut-Torn-Crushed)*. If this process has been used to gather tea for the bag, the insignia *C.T.C.* will be shown on the tea company's packaging.

The advantage of using tea bags, however, is their time and labor convenience.

They infuse faster and the disposable bags eliminate the need to remove loose leaves from teapots and cups.

Steeping time for tea bags depends on a variety of factors such as the particular tea blend, the manufacturing process used on the leaves, and the grade of the leaf particles. As a rule, green tea infuses faster than black tea and Oolong infusion time is somewhere between the two. If tea bags contain the smallest-grade particles— fannings and dust—they will infuse faster and produce a lower-quality cup than tea bags containing the broken pieces of higher-grade teas such as Broken Pekoe. Tea drinkers are advised to read the instructions on the company's packaging before brewing. As a general guide, use 1 tea bag per 6 oz. of boiling water.

Western research indicates that a bag of black tea should be infused for five minutes, no longer. The five-minute mark is when the harsher or more bitter-tasting polyphenols from the leaves start to be emitted into the water. Tea bags should not be pressed with a spoon against the side of a cup or pot to infuse the tea faster or to squeeze out the drops, as the polyphenols left in the bag produce a bitter taste. After infusing tea, lift the bag out with a spoon and place on a plate to catch the drips.

Although the majority of people in the Western world use tea bags when brewing tea these days, it should be noted that good-quality whole-leaf teas produce a better cup. For this reason, many tea connoisseurs worldwide would not consider tea bags their "cup of tea."

INSTANT TEA

As if tea was not instant enough, it is available in instant form. In keeping with a faster-paced society, tea making can be made even easier by spooning freeze-dried tea granules into a cup of water and stirring.

The soluble powder is prepared using a highly concentrated brew of tea from which the water is removed by a special drying process. Soluble tea has actually been around since the 1930s, but it was not until the 1960s that instant cold-water teas became popular and began to be perceived as a marketable alternative to soft drinks. Canned ice tea is usually made from instant tea.

Nestea suggests the following measurements for their instant tea:

For iced tea: 1 rounded tsp. per 8 oz. glass of water *or* 5 rounded tsp. per 5 cups water to make a pitcher-full.

For hot tea: 1 level tsp. per 6 oz. hot water.

Thomas J. Lipton Inc., in promoting its instant Red Rose Tea, suggests using 1 level tsp. per cup boiling water or adjust to taste. Stir and sip.

Storing Tea

Fresh tea leaves are a key ingredient in making a successful cup of tea. Here are some suggestions for storing your tea to keep it fresh for brewing:

1. Store the tea in a clean, dry, seal-tight container, free from foreign materials and odors.

2. Keep small amounts of tea in your tea caddy so you can replenish the stock more frequently. Make sure the remaining tea leaves at the bottom of the caddy are removed, otherwise they will become stale, affecting the added fresh tea.

3. Use a dry spoon to measure tea from the caddy. Seal the caddy immediately after removing the quantity of tea you desire.

Note: When buying tea it is often impossible to know its age from the time it was harvested. If properly stored, black teas may remain flavorful for up to two years. Green teas are best used within six months after picking. Tea bags will deteriorate faster because they may contain lower grades of tea.

Decaffeinated Tea

Whether a person chooses to drink a decaffeinated tea or not is a matter of personal preference. The main reason a person would drink decaffeinated tea is because he or she is sensitive to the effects of caffeine. By American Food and Drug Administration standards, decaffeinated tea must not contain more than 5 mg. of caffeine per cup.

Decaffeinated tea leaves unfortunately produce a flatter-tasting tea. Decaf tea also lacks the "aliveness" and intensity of regularly processed tea. This loss of taste quality in the cup is due to the timing of decaffeination. Decaffeination is carried out after the tea leaves have already been through the manufacturing process; consequently, decaffeination adds one more heat process.

The most common decaffeinating solvent is ethyl acetate, a substance that occurs naturally in some fruits. Chemically, ethyl acetate breaks down into alcohol and acetic acid. Both these components are considered safe for use in decaffeinating by the FDA.

A person sensitive to the effects of caffeine can experiment by substituting decaf tea for regular tea leaves in homemade flavored tea drinks. Herbs, spices, and/or

THE TEA BOOK

fruits can be added to decaf tea leaves when steeping. With a little imagination, decaf drinkers can still enjoy a flavored or scented tea after dinner or during a cozy get-together with friends.

Flavored Teas

Unfortunately, some of the flavored teas one buys on the market are not flavored with natural ingredients. Flavorings vary from chemical additives, which are structurally similar to the flavor being imitated, to very artificial flavorings, which simulate a particular flavor on the taste buds. The flavors are usually sprayed onto the tea leaves while the leaves are in a heated state.

There are many teas, however, that do have natural flavoring ingredients, such as Earl Grey tea with its oil of Bergamot, or the many Chinese blossom-flavored teas (e.g., jasmine tea). Tea drinkers should read the labels on the packaging to ascertain which ingredients have been added.

To ensure enjoyment of naturally flavored teas, flavor your own favorite tea-leaf blends with your choice of flower petals, citrus rinds, fruits, and/or spices.

Tea Things

Many accessories have been designed to make the serving of tea easier (if such a thing is possible) and more enjoyable. Tea *equipage,* as it used to be called, is often aesthetically pleasing as well as practical. Here are a few of the tea things available for the tea drinker.

A **tea caddy** is a seal-tight container designed for storing tea leaves. The name comes from the Malay word *kati,* which was a weight measure of 1⅔ lb. If tea leaves are stored in a tightly sealed container in a cool dry place, they will last for up to two years. The earliest tea caddies were created in sets of two, one caddy for green tea and the other for Bohea.

A **teaspoon** measures the amount of tea leaves to be used when making tea. Usually 1 tsp. of tea leaves is used per 6 oz. of water. Other teaspoons are used for stirring tea in the cup, when milk, sugar, and/or other ingredients have been added to it.

A **tea cozy** is an artistically crafted (knitted, crocheted, quilted) cover that has been fashioned to fit a teapot. Its purpose is to help keep the tea hot. Tea cozies are usually very decorative and come in a variety of shapes.

To many people, teatime also means indulging in tea snacks and pastries. These are usually served on tea ware specifically designed for this purpose. For the last three centuries, a set of **pastry plates** has been considered an essential part of the tea service. The plates are often family heirlooms. Examples of tea-service dishes are small pastry or dessert plates, cake plates, and bread and butter plates.

Tea-bag tongs are used for lifting the tea bag from a pot or cup and/or for squeezing out more liquid or essence from the tea bag. Some people consider squeezing tea bags taboo, because it forces more polyphenols into the tea, giving it a bitter taste. Others, like the Australians, prefer to squeeze out that extra little bit of essence into the cup, as they prefer the bitter taste.

A tea bag squeezer prevents a wet tea bag from creating a mess as it is transferred to the **stop bowl.** This is a plate or bowl designed to hold the used tea bag or tea ball.

A **lemon squeezer** is a small gadget that can hold a wedge of lemon. It squeezes lemon into the tea without getting juice on a person's fingers, thereby preserving proper etiquette.

Sugar tongs are used to transfer sugar cubes from the sugar bowl to the teacup. The earliest sugar tongs resembled fire tongs. The one-piece sugar tong, similar to that used today, first appeared in 1780.

Tea and Your Health

Considering that tea has been a part of our civilization for over four and a half millennia, it is surprising that Western research on the health effects of tea on the human body is still in its infancy. At this very late date in tea's history, some Western researchers are starting to share the Oriental cultures' long-held beliefs that tea's effects are medicinal. Tea, and in particular green tea, it seems from modern research, may be healthy for us.

Evidence is starting to accumulate indicating that green tea may possibly be cancer inhibiting. Repeated studies have been done feeding tea instead of water to mice and then exposing them to a wide variety of cancer-inducing agents, with these mice developing fewer cancers than control-group mice. Research in both the United States and Japan has further demonstrated that tea-drinking mice show few incidences of cancers of the lungs, liver, stomach, and skin. Tea-drinking mice exposed to NNK, a major carcinogen in cigarette smoke, were found to develop fewer cancerous tumors than non-tea-drinking mice. It is thought then that tea drinking may possibly account for the very low incidence of lung cancer among the Japanese people even though Japan is a heavy cigarette-consuming nation.

Japanese researchers have more recently isolated in green tea a chemical that they believe is one of the agents that possesses cancer-inhibiting properties. Studies show that when the chemical extract, called EGCG (epigallocatechin gallate), was given to mice, their skin was found to be resistant to the effects of carcinogenic chemicals.

Many of tea's other inherent substances are also being closely scrutinized by the science and health professions. Caffeine, one of the most witch-hunted substances of the seventies and eighties, falls into this category. Caffeine stimulates the central nervous system and large muscles. It dilates blood vessels, increases heart rate, increases metabolism, and helps to move wastes through the body. In extreme quantities, caffeine can be toxic, producing irritability, nervousness, sleeplessness, and even mental confusion. On the more positive side, it is the dilation of the blood vessels that provides a "cooling effect" in hot climates.

Canada's Food Guide states that "for most people 400-450 mg. of caffeine per day does not increase the risk of heart disease, hypertension or have adverse effects on pregnancy or the fetus." At the same time, the Food Guide also advises that it is important to moderate caffeine intake, particularly during pregnancy and breast feeding. Caffeine will penetrate the placenta, and also will appear in breast milk.

One must consume two to three cups of tea for every cup of coffee to receive the same amount of caffeine. The reason for this difference is that, for a cup of beverage, fewer tea leaves than coffee beans are needed. Drinking tea instead of coffee seems to be the obvious choice for anyone wanting to cut down on caffeine consumption.

The amount of caffeine in tea can vary depending on where the tea was grown, the manufacturing processing used, the length of time the tea is brewed, and the particular blend of tea. Black teas and Oolong teas contain more caffeine than green teas because of the fermentation process they undergo. Roughly speaking, black tea contains just over 2 percent caffeine by weight.

Caffeine-conscious consumers can obtain less caffeine in their cup by infusing their tea leaves for a shorter period of time. Smaller leaves or leaf grades extract caffeine into the water faster. Following are the caffeine quantity approximations for teas with various brewing times.

Caffeine in a 5-Oz. Cup

Black tea, loose leaves or tea bag
    (brewed 1 minute) ....9-33 mg.

Black tea, loose leaves (brewed 3 minutes)..................................20-46 mg.

Black tea, tea bag (brewed 5 minutes or longer) ....46-108 mg.

Instant tea (8 oz.) ....12-28 mg.

Oolong tea, loose leaves (maximum infusion time) ....12-55 mg.

Green tea, loose leaves (maximum infusion time) ....8-16 mg.

Iced tea (12-oz. can)..22-36 mg.

Decaffeinated tea ....4 mg.

The polyphenols in tea are being studied for their possible antiviral and antibacterial effects, which might account for the folkloric history of tea being a treatment for flus. Already it is known that polyphenols are useful as a digestive stimulant and for treating diarrhea, with a fair warning that too much may cause constipation. Adversely, they deplete the body of vitamins B and C and minerals like iron and calcium. It has been suggested that adding a small amount of lemon or orange juice to the tea would compensate for this depleting effect. The extra vitamin C from the citrus fruits would aid in the body's absorption of the minerals.

Theophylline, which occurs in small amounts in tea, is being studied for its effects on the human body. Theophylline is a stimulant substance used to treat asthma. It is helpful in opening up the bronchioles of the lungs, but in larger dosages, it can cause irritation of the stomach and the intestines and can even cause nausea. Theophylline when combined with caffeine can cause a nervous reaction.

On a lighter note, tea contains fluoride, which has been found to be a major factor in reducing tooth decay. There may be other ingredients in tea that inhibit plaque formation. It has been suggested that one and a half cups of black or one cup of green tea infused for three minutes may be the quantity a person needs to drink in a day to reduce tooth decay.

Next to water, tea has been described as the most universal beverage of mankind. Throughout its history, tea drinking has been viewed as a peaceful occupation by all cultures that have embraced it. Now scientific research is indicating that tea may just have that "calming effect" it has long been touted to have. The suspected contributors to the calming effect are the flavonoids found in tea.

In addition, research now suggests that tea may be helpful in stabilizing blood sugar. It may contribute to lowering blood pressure and blood cholesterol.

The research into the effects of tea on the body is still far from being conclusive, but it is creating a lot of excitement and optimism in the scientific community. The results of many studies thus far are pointing strongly towards a definite health benefit from drinking tea, and in particular green tea. It may well turn out that tea will be considered one of the healthiest beverages of our time.

Two Dutch women having tea use saucers to drink from (Schotel Drinken).
This method of drinking tea was common in the 1600s.

Traditional Tea Recipes from Around the World

As tea migrated from its native home in China to other parts of the world, each new region embraced the simple drink. Many added their own flavoring ingredients, most of which were specific to their native lands. In India, traditionally the land of spices, the inhabitants added aniseeds, cardamom pods, fennel, ginger, peppercorns, and a myriad of other spices to the pot when boiling their tea. In Tibet, tea was mixed with rancid yak butter and barley meal. The mixture became a substantial part of the Tibetans' daily food sustenance.

When tea finally made its way across Manchuria into Russia, the Russians became so enamored with the new brew that they began sweetening it with preserves made from their favorite fruits. The Russians also added lemon slices and lemon peels to black tea, thereby introducing to the world that light lemony taste and fragrance with which all of us have become so familiar when we enjoy "tea with lemon" or "tea with a twist."

A multitude of brewing variations developed around the world, all of which ultimately affected the taste of the tea. Methods of preparation ranged from the Australian outbacker who boiled river or spring water and then steeped the tea leaves in it for hours over a charcoal fire in a can called a *billy*; to the Brit who arrogantly insisted that there was such a thing as a "perfect cup of tea," achieved by taking the brew water hot off the boil and steeping the tea leaves in it for a prescribed five minutes . . . no longer. Perfect perhaps, but that would have been an insult to the Moroccans, who believed that variations in tea making were part of the whole tea-drinking experience. To this day in Morocco, it is boasted that "no two cups of tea ever taste the same."

Distinct customs surrounding the tea drinking itself also developed differently throughout the world. In Japan, for example, there is a ritualistic silence among guests while they participate in the Japanese Tea Ceremony. The tea master and the guests bow reverently to each other before and after drinking tea in a room that has been specially constructed for this purpose.

And while silence speaks respectfully during a Japanese Tea Ceremony, in England, only half a globe away, one can almost "see" the gossip fly during the afternoon teatimes. Reputations can still be made or broken by what is brewed up and consumed in these seemingly innocuous gatherings. In fact, British novelist Henry Fielding (1707-54) was probably right when he proclaimed almost three centuries ago that "love and scandal are the best sweeteners of tea."

When circling the globe, one soon discovers that the assortment of tea drinks and the variations for the making and enjoying of them are as unique as the countries from which they originated. For this reason, it is the author's hope that the recipes contained in the following pages will provide tea lovers with the opportunity to experience a variety of teas and tea-drinking customs from around the world.

AFGHANISTAN

Afghanistan is a predominantly tea-drinking country. Both green and black teas are enjoyed. Varieties of tea leaves imported mainly from India can be found piled "mountain high" in baskets at marketplaces.

Tora chai (black tea) is the preferred breakfast beverage in Afghanistan. It accompanies *parathas* (fried chapatties) and fried eggs. Black tea is also sipped throughout the day. Afghanis prefer a sweet tea using jaggery (an unrefined brown sugar made from the sap of various palms) or white sugar.

Company is always served black tea with accompaniments like cookies or dried fruits (apricots, raisins) and nuts (almonds, pistachios, walnuts).

Porcelain ware in Afghanistan can have a wonderful antique look. This is because, when the porcelain ware is broken, it is not thrown away. Instead it is mended with brass tacks, nimbly placed right through the tea ware, straddling the breaks and pulling the broken pieces together.

Chaikhana (teahouses) in Afghanistan are usually small roadside establishments. These adobe-type structures are about six feet by six feet with mud floors and corrugated-metal roofs. A few tables and benches may be placed both inside and outside a *chaikhana*. Strangers sit all together at the tables and chat. Children often serve the tea. At the back of most teahouses, a charcoal fire is maintained all day long. Tea is kept constantly on the brew.

Women are not allowed to visit teahouses as Afghanis believe a teahouse is not a decent enough establishment to serve their womenfolk in. Male customers do not spend long periods of time there either. A customer will drop in briefly while en route to another destination.

TORA CHAI (BLACK TEA)

Black tea is served in porcelain cups and saucers (pyale au priche). The usual size of serving is about 5-6 oz.

2 tsp. black tea leaves
6 oz. water
1 cup milk
2-4 tsp. sugar

Place all the ingredients in a *chanek* (aluminum pot) on high heat and bring them to a boil. Strain the mixture through a metal cup strainer into cups. Serves 2.

ADRAK SERA CHAI (TEA WITH GINGER)

During the wintertime, powdered ginger may be added to black tea. Ginger improves the body's circulation. To a large pot of tora chai (8 cups), add ½-1 tsp. powdered ginger, when boiling the tea leaves. Serves 8.
Note: For 1 cup of tora chai, add ⅛-¼ tsp. powdered ginger.

SHIN CHAI (GREEN TEA)

Shin chai is sweetened green tea served on special occasions such as weddings or after full-course meals. It is also given as a soother when one is ill, most likely because green tea, unlike black tea, has less caffeine and is not served with milk.

2 tsp. green tea leaves
Sugar to taste
6 oz. boiling water

Place tea and sugar in a 2-cup-size chanek. Pour water into the pot and infuse the tea for 5 minutes. Then strain into 3-oz. bowl-like drinking cups similar to those in China. Serves 2.

ELACHI SERA CHAI (GREEN TEA WITH CARDAMOM)

To the above green tea recipe, add 3 or 4 cardamom pods per 6 oz. water to the teapot when steeping the tea leaves. Crush the cardamom pods just before adding them.

SHIR CHAI (MILK TEA)

Make sweet green tea by the usual method (see above). Cool the tea by pouring it back and forth from the cups to the teapot. Cool milk is then added to the tea.

Note: Cow or buffalo milk in Afghanistan is not homogenized, so all the milk has to be boiled before use. Milk that cannot be stored in refrigerators is stored in terra-cotta pots. The terra-cotta helps to keep the milk at a lower temperature.

AFRICA (NORTH)

Tea in some regions of North Africa is made in huge metal kettles heated on charcoal fires. When the water in the kettle begins to boil, handfuls of tea leaves are thrown in. The tea is boiled for a good 15 minutes to make a heavy-bodied brew. The brew is then poured back and forth between the kettle and another large container until it is aerated and frothy. In contrast to the large size of the kettle, the tea glasses are tiny, about 3 inches in height.

SAHARAN DESERT TEA

Tea making is a favorite activity of the Saharans and they "do it up" in fine style. Teatimes take place several times a day in the Sahara and they are seldom ever missed. Even if a Saharan is in transit through the desert for the day, he will pack his tea, sugar, a pot, and tea glasses with him wherever he goes.

The small Saharan tea glass plays an integral part of the tea-making process. To make tea, fill a 3-inch glass halfway with Chinese Gunpowder tea. Put the tea leaves from the glass into a small brass pot. Fill 2 tea glasses with boiling water. Pour the boiling water from the tea glasses over the top of the tea leaves. Then throw

out the water, making sure the wet tea leaves remain attached to the pot. (This process washes the tea leaves.)

Add mint leaves (preferably 4) and 3 tea-glassfuls of sugar to the teapot. (If sugar is not available, pieces of sugarcane are added to the pot.)

Pour 3 glassfuls of boiling water over the mint, sugar, and tea leaves. Steep the mixture for 1 minute. Then pour the tea back and forth between the glasses and the small brass pot "three times" with the last pour ending up in the glasses. Serves 3.

Saharan tea is one of the "sweetest" tea drinks in the world.

LE THE

Living under a hot sun, Algerians stay hydrated and cool with this pleasant-tasting, mint-flavored tea. Skilled tea servers in Algeria usually create a visual "show" while pouring tea. Holding the teapot or kettle as high as two feet above the glasses, they pour the tea downwards in a steady stream without spilling more than a drop. It is customary for Algerians to drink three glasses of tea at every sitting, so this display is re-created time and time again.

1 tbsp. green tea leaves
1 tbsp. mint leaves
¾ cup sugar
3 cups boiling water

Place tea leaves, mint, and sugar in teapot. Pour water over ingredients. Cover teapot and steep tea for 5 minutes. Pour into 3-oz. glasses. Serves 9.

ARMENIA

TEY

In Armenia, tea is drunk during the wintertime usually for medicinal purposes. Milk is not added.

6 cups water
2 large cinnamon sticks
A few cloves
8 tsp. tea leaves
Sugar to taste

Place water, cinnamon sticks, and a few cloves in a pot. Bring the spiced water to a boil, then turn down the heat and simmer ingredients for 5 minutes. Remove the spice water from the heat and stir in the tea leaves. Steep the ingredients for a few minutes, then strain spicy tea into another pot or into cups. Sweeten the tea with as much sugar as desired. Serves 6-8. This recipe may be halved.

AUSTRALIA

DUNKER TEA

The Aussies are tea-bag dunkers. Tea-bag dunking is done by bobbing the tea bag up and down in the teacup. The tea bag is removed when the tea is the desired strength.

Some Aussies are known for "helping" their tea bags along. They take a spoon and apply pressure to the top of the tea bag, forcing the tea essences to infuse into the water faster. Squeezing the tea bag emits more polyphenols into the water, resulting in a slightly bitter tasting tea.

Mainstream Aussies drink their tea "white" (with milk). Sugar is added, if desired. Australia is one of the foremost tea-consuming nations per capita in the world. Most of the teas drunk there are imported from Java, Sumatra, and Papua New Guinea.

BILLY BREW (OUTBACKER TEA)

Everyone has heard of the infamous Aussie outbackers, who have their own life-style suited to the raw and challenging elements of the outback. Tea making for the outbackers is also unique, varying from their urban Australian counterparts.

To make Outbacker Tea, add a handful of tea leaves to a large can (billy) of boiling water. Boil or heat the tea until it is one nasty dark-colored potion. Outbackers like their brew s-t-r-o-n-g and bitter. So if you like the taste of tea to hang off of your tongue, or to cling to your gut, Billy Brew will accomplish this feat.

The billy has a wire handle attached to it, so it can be hung over a fire. Customarily, an outbacker will leave his billy, filled with tea leaves and water, either hanging on a tripod over the coals of his morning fire or sitting on the coals before he leaves for his long day's work in the bush. When he returns in the evening, he rekindles his fire and reheats the billy, which is brim full with the day-long-steeped Billy Brew. Loads of sugar and/or a gum-tree leaf (eucalyptus) are added to the tea just before serving to sweeten it, flavor it, and take the edge off the bitterness.

Gloves are commonly used to handle the billy because it is very hot to touch. For a little show in front of friends, an outbacker may take the billy and swing it at full arm's length around and around in circles to settle the tea leaves in a hurry before serving up the tea.

This ever-loved, charcoal-burnt, bent, and dented billy is celebrated in the Australian patriotic song, "Waltzing Matilda":

> And he sang as he watched and waited till
> his billy boiled,
> "You'll come a-waltzing Matilda with me."

AUSTRIA

Tee for Austrians really means "tea with spirits." In Austria, tea is drunk mainly with liquor in it.

It is interesting to note that tea drinking in this country is seasonal. Tea is served with its companion alcohol mainly during the winter months.

Tea is also served at *Gasthauses* (guesthouses) and inns for hikers in the Alps. There is customarily a picnic table set outside at each one. To be served tea, one merely needs to sit down at the table and soon the host/ess will appear with the spirited drink.

TEE MIT RUM (TEA WITH RUM)

Add rum to tea or add hot tea to rum.

TEE MIT SLIVOVITZ (TEA WITH SLIVOVITZ)

Yugoslavian blue-plum brandy, Slivovitz, a favorite of Austrians, is often added to tea. Plum brandy is also made in other central European countries.

RUSSISCHER TEE (RUSSIAN TEA)

Austrians import their tea from Russia. Loose tea is put in a *Tee Ei* (tea egg) and infused in the cup. It is served with pastries.

Note: Although Austrians are mainly coffee drinkers, *Kaffeehauses* offer tea as well as coffee. Tea is served "straight" or with milk *(Tee mit Milch)*.

BOLIVIA

Tea is imported to Bolivia from the major tea-growing countries of Sri Lanka, India, and China. Import teas by major tea companies such as Horniman's and Lipton are also available. Black tea in Bolivia is drunk very sweet; it is not unusual to see a Bolivian drop four or even five teaspoons of *azuc*ar (sugar) into his or her tea. Brown sugar is not favored, even though Bolivia has its own sugarcane plantations. Also, milk is rarely ever added to tea, despite Bolivia's dairy industry.

To make tea, ceramic *teteras,* teapots, are used by some people, but by and large the mainstream method is to infuse tea bags for several minutes in ceramic cups or metal mugs. Then lots of sugar is added.

Bolivia is both a coffee- and a tea-drinking country. Tea or coffee is drunk at breakfast, accompanied by pieces of bread and cheese. Around four o'clock in the afternoon, Bolivians take a tea break *(té de las)*.

Tea is drunk more by people in the urban areas. People from the rural areas are not as interested in consuming tea-leaf tea, preferring instead *maté de coca* (coca-leaf tea) and herbal teas.

TE CON LIMON

A slice of lemon is floated on top of a cup of sugar-sweetened tea.

TE CON TE

Night workers such as taxi drivers, truck drivers, factory workers, and mine workers aid themselves in "staying awake" by adding an ounce or two of cane alcohol or *agua ardiente* (grape brandy) to their tea. Students often fortify themselves during their long hours of studying with *té con té* accompanied by coca leaves, which they chew. The belief that cane alcohol, with its depressant quality, can keep workers awake throughout the night may be a Bolivian cultural myth. The coca leaves, on the other hand, do provide a stimulant effect, and both contribute towards the sociability that can be seen on Bolivian urban streets at night.

BRAZIL

Brazil, being the largest coffee producer in the world, is primarily a coffee-drinking nation. However, tea drinking has been increasing in popularity since the early seventies among the middle class and in the wealthier areas. Tea is now grown in the Bahia area of Brazil. The Bahia is a well-known, highly productive coffee-growing region, with a strong African influence dating back to the slave-trading days.

Tea drinking has not spread among the masses as of yet. However, ladies out for a day's shopping may stop and enjoy an "afternoon tea." Teahouses called *copos de chá,* which means "cups of tea," have sprung up in the cities of Brazil. Here one can order a cup of tea and a Danish pastry. Both green and black teas are available, served in porcelain cups.

Tea is served with milk, or cream and sugar if preferred. Brazil has large sugar-cane and dairy industries. In a *copo de chá,* you may ask for:

Chá com leite: tea with milk.
Chá sem leite: tea without milk.
Chá com azúcar: tea with sugar.

A damp sugar that melts faster than the conventional granulated sugar is used in Brazil. Tea is made and drunk the same way as it is in the United States.

CANADA

Canadians have been large consumers of tea since their early pioneer days. While the American Revolution was taking place in the 1770s and many American colonists were boycotting tea as a symbol of their defiance, some colonists refrained from following their neighbors and, instead, remained loyal to the monarchy, the British Empire, and, of course, the tea-drinking traditions. The Loyalists emigrating en masse to Canada from the American colonies probably helped to ingrain further the tea-drinking custom in Canada.

These days, Canadians consume over seven billion cups of tea annually, the tea drinking being evenly shared by men and women. Canadians drink black tea, usually made with Orange Pekoe grade tea bags. Tea is served straight (without milk or sugar), light (with milk or 10 percent butterfat cream), and light with sugar (with 1 tsp. of sugar and milk). Clover honey, white sugar, brown sugar, raw sugar, or artificial sugar may be added to tea as a sweetener. Most restaurants offer a variety of sweeteners to choose from.

CAMPFIRE TEA

Heat the tea water in a large can on the hot coals of your campfire. When the water is hot and steaming, remove the can from the fire. Wear heavy gloves, so you will not burn your hands. Add a few tea bags to the water and infuse them for several minutes. Pour the hot tea into your campfire cup and sweeten it with sugar, if desired.

Note: Coffee tins or large soup cans work well for heating the water.

GLACIER-WATER TEA
(ROCKY MOUNTAIN FALLS TEA)

This tea is made with the waters from melting snow or glaciers, rushing or dripping down the rock faces of the Rocky Mountains, en route to small streams and mighty rivers. If you are from a region of Canada or a part of the world where you cannot hang a pot out with your hand and fill it up with ice-cold mountain water, you'll have to purchase a bottle of it from a specialty store.

Campfire Tea.

Make tea in the usual way by infusing a tea bag in 6-8 oz. boiling mountain water for 3-5 minutes. This tea is wonderful when it is steeped outdoors over a hot fire and sipped in the cool mountain air.

MOUNTAIN CLIMBER'S TEA

On your next mountain hike, take along a flask filled with a double-strength tea. When stopping to rest by a cool waterfall or stream, take out your camper's cup and dip it in the cool waters to chill the cup. Empty the cup. Now pour a little of the strong tea into the cup and fill it the rest of the way with the cold mountain water. This is a cool refreshing tea, the taste of which you'll never forget.

SUNSHINE TEA/SUN TEA

Fill a quart jar with water and insert 4 tea bags. Seal the jar with a tight lid. Leave jar under the shade of a tree all day while you are hiking. Or, for a faster infusion, place the jar in an unshaded area, so it will be subject to the noonday sun.

You may heat this tea later, adding water if you prefer to dilute its strength. Serves 4.

For a cold tea, set a jar or other seal-tight container in the rocks at the edge of a river. Secure the container with heavier rocks. The tea will be cooled by the cold river waters. Watch your step when retrieving your tea.

CHILE

Tea drinking began in northern Chile during the British settlement years. When the British were mining *salitre* (an ingredient in fertilizers) in the Atacama Desert of Chile, the Chilean work force they employed were paid with vouchers instead of cash. The vouchers unfortunately could only be redeemed "at the British store." Here imported teas were available; thus it was that the mine workers and their families were introduced to tea and the tea-drinking customs of the British.

Needless to say, tea in Chile is drunk the same way as in England. Originally, loose black tea was used for infusions, but in the early 1950s when Tetley introduced the tea bag to the English market, the tea-bag revolution made its way to Chile as well. Tea is made by infusing a tea bag in a *taza* (cup) or aluminum *tetera* (teapot). Water just off the boil is poured over the tea bag.

The Chileans produce their own porcelain tea ware, thus tea is drunk from beautiful *tazas y platillos* (cups and saucers). The water for tea is heated in a *tetera* or in an enameled pot on a gas stove. Wooden potbelly stoves are used in the rural areas to heat the tea water. A straight infusion is preferred by Chileans; milk is not usually added.

During the afternoon in Chile, there is a *tomar onces,* a teatime, between the hours of four and five. Favorite accompaniments to tea are cookies, cakes, *alfajones* (wafers with condensed-milk fillings), or *chilenitos* (sweet buns, covered with icing).

TE CON LECHE

This tea is similar to the English version of Cambric Tea (see "England"). A small amount of strongly brewed tea is added to a cupful of heated milk. The amount of tea added to the hot milk varies according to personal preference. Serves 1.

TE CON CANELA (TEA WITH CINNAMON)

Place a cinnamon stick into the teapot when steeping tea.

TE CON LIMON (TEA WITH LEMON)

A thin lemon slice is floated on top of a cup of sweetened tea.

TE CON PISCO

Pisco is Peruvian brandy made from grapes. It is distilled in paraffin-wax-lined containers so as not to take on foreign tastes. Generally speaking, however, Pisco is a harsh-tasting alcohol.

Tea with Pisco is drunk more commonly by students, workers in the mines, and evening and night-shift workers such as taxi drivers. Supposedly, it helps get one through the working hours.

Add an ounce of Pisco to a cup of tea.

MI CHA GAO CHA
(RICE-TEA-CAKE TEA)

Perhaps no one really knows when and where tea drinking began. However, by the fifth century in China, a recipe on how to make rice tea cakes appeared in a Chinese dictionary, the *Kuang-Ya*.

To make these early reddish-colored tea cakes, the tea leaves were mixed with rice and the two ingredients were baked or roasted. The resulting cakes were then pounded into little pieces and placed in a white-glazed earthenware jar. Boiling water was poured over them to infuse. Once an infusion was obtained, other ingredients such as onion and ginger were added to the souplike tea broth to improve upon its taste.

Tea during this period was utilized mainly for medicinal purposes.

CHA GAO CHA (TEA-CAKE TEA)

Lu Yu, in his famous work, *Ch'a Ching* (A.D. 780), advised, "To one pint of water, add no more than a square inch of tea." The "square inch" of tea, of course, was cut from tea cakes. During the T'ang Dynasty (618-906), the Chinese stored their tea in compressed blocks of tea called "tea cakes." These were made by crushing tea leaves into powder, making a paste, and then molding the paste into tea cakes. Tea for the pot or cup was obtained by shaving off the desired amount of tea.

A tea recipe mentioned by Lu Yu in the *Ch'a Ching* describes pressing the tea leaves into a cake. The cake was then roasted, shredded, and pieces of it were boiled in water.

To the tea pieces other flavorings such as cinnamon, onion, salt, orange peels, peppermint, and/or ginger were added. All the ingredients were brewed together. Then tea was served in blue- or white-glazed earthenware cups typical of the T'ang Dynasty. Lu Yu advised using the blue earthenware cups because the blue enhanced the color of the tea.

Of this wondrous tea, the eighth-century T'ang poet and Tea Master Lu T'ung wrote:

The first cup moistens my lips and throat, the second cup breaks my loneliness, the third cup searches my barren entrails but to find therein some five thousand volumes of odd ideographs. The fourth cup raises a slight perspiration—all the wrong of life passes through my pores. At the fifth cup I am purified; the sixth cup calls me to the realms of immortals. The seventh cup—ah, but I could take no more! I only feel the breath of cool wind that rises in my sleeves. Where is Horaisan? Let me ride on this sweet breeze and waft away thither.

Note: Lu T'ung was revered by the Chinese for being one of their best connoisseurs of tea. Apparently he filled almost all of the hours of his adult life with writing poems and drinking tea.

FEN CHA (WHIPPED TEA)

The Sung Dynasty (960-1271) is considered one of the most productive periods in Chinese history, characterized by cultural and artistic development. Teahouses were created during this period to provide a unique and specialized setting just for the serving of tea. Tea was drunk in a ceremonial fashion from wide, shallow, saucerlike bowls called *zhan*. The bowls were heavy, and dark brown or blue-black colored. The tea water was heated in a bottle-shaped, earthenware container called a *ping*.

It was during the Sung Dynasty that the Chinese developed whipped powdered tea, and the tea drink became appreciated and consumed for the taste of the tea itself. Loose tea leaves came into popular usage. Salt and other ingredients formerly used to flavor tea were no longer added.

To make a whipped tea, use a powdered green tea or grind green tea leaves into powder form. Put 1 tsp. of powdered tea into a small drinking bowl. Add a small amount of water to the powdered tea and mix it into a smooth paste. Then add boiling water to the paste and dilute it into a thinner tea. This tea is usually whipped with a bamboo whisk until it becomes frothy.

MONGOL CONQUEST TEA

During the Yuan Dynasty of the Mongols (1271-1368), tea was still drunk from saucerlike bowls. It was made by placing a small amount of tea leaves and a small amount of boiling water in the bowl. The tea and the water were mixed into a thick infusion. Then more boiling water was added to dilute it into a drinkable tea. It was almost impossible not to ingest some of the tea leaves using this preparation.

LIU CHA (GREEN TEA)

In the Ming Dynasty (1368-1644), loose green tea was becoming more common than cake tea. The processes for manufacturing black teas and Oolongs were created. During the latter part of this period the Western world was introduced to tea from China.

During the Ming Dynasty, the Yi-Hsing teapot became commonplace, replacing the long-standing usage of the *zhan* for making tea in. With the further development of Chinese ceramics, the Yi-Hsing teapots were created in hundreds of shapes—geometric ones like cubes and rectangles, natural ones like flowers, pumpkins, insects, etc. These were the first pots with handles and spouts. (Also during this period, smaller cups were used, replacing the wide-rimmed saucerlike bowls.) The earthenware water bottle, the *ping,* however, was still used to heat the water.

A late-seventeenth-century Yi-Hsing stoneware teapot.

The following is how tea was made during the Ming Dynasty. Place the green tea leaves in a teapot full of boiling water. After a few seconds, pour the light infusion from the pot into teacups. Then, take the liquid from the cups and pour it back into the pot. Cover the pot and allow the leaves to settle before serving.

TEA IN THE CH'ING DYNASTY (1644-1911)

During this period, many parts of the Western world became enamored with tea and with the glazed earthenware from China. Chinese Yi-Hsing teapots and *chá zhong* (teacups) were in high demand on the Continent. The exported teacups were made of porcelain as well as earthenware.

Tea made with loose leaves became the standard throughout most of the tea-drinking world.

Ch'ing Dynasty enameled porcelain teapot and teacup.

TEA IN THE TWENTIETH CENTURY

The earthenware Yi-Hsing teapots made in the Kiangsu are still considered by the Chinese as the best for making tea. Connoisseurs claim that the pores of the earthenware pots absorb the fragrance of tea, thus adding to the taste and the drinking experience itself. For this reason, many Chinese people believe teapots should not be scoured.

Most Chinese like to possess their own Yi-Hsing teapot *(chá hu),* and a set of teacups to serve tea to their guests.

Following are the contemporary methods of making tea in China. After green tea is made in a teapot, a small amount of tea is poured into each cup. Hot water is poured over the wet tea leaves in the teapot and the new infusion is shared equally among the cups. The advantages of using this pouring method are that all of the teacups will be filled to the brim at approximately the same time and the strength of infusion will be almost the same in each cup.

Another method is to place loose tea leaves in a teacup and pour boiling water over the leaves. The tea is drunk when the leaves have settled to the bottom of the cup. Several infusion waters may be used on the same green tea leaves. This tea is made the same way when using a teapot.

Tea using the above method can also be made in a *gài wán,* a handleless bowl-shaped cup with a lid and saucer. The lid is placed over the cup while the tea leaves are infusing.

In some areas of China, tea glasses with lids are now replacing the handleless teacups. Glasses have the advantage of displaying the fine infusion colors of some of the green teas. Mugs with handles and lids called *chá bei* are now available in Shanghai and southern China.

Green tea is far more popular in China than is black tea. As a rule, black tea leaves are only infused once. Most Chinese prefer a straight infusion—milk or sugar is rarely added. Tea is drunk at any time of the day, depending on personal preference.

There are remarkable stories and legends surrounding the many beautiful names given to China's teas. The following are but a few of the hundreds of names bestowed on teas: Bright Virtue, Cloud Mist, Dragon's Beard, Handful of Snow, Silver Needle, and Water Nymph.

TEAHOUSES IN CHINA

The Chinese have always been known for their teahouses. Upon arriving in China, a foreigner would go straight to the public teahouse for tea and *dim sum* (breakfast served from six o'clock till noon). After the Communist Revolution this long-standing and most-loved tradition declined. Only now, with China beginning to develop a larger market economy, is the teahouse regaining favor for the ordinary Chinese, many of whom were not raised with the teahouse tradition.

A lidded gài wán (5 oz.). A larger gài wán can be used like a teapot for pouring tea into small cups. It can also be used as a drinking cup itself.

Early teahouses served mainly monks and aristocrats. Some of the more famous and ancient houses are architectural works of art. They are usually found near springs and rivers in areas where tea is cultivated.

THE CHINESE ART OF TEA

Chinese connoisseurs believe that the art of drinking tea is not based solely on the type of tea selected and the method of preparing it. Rather, to be considered an "artistic experience," tea drinking should combine the following many fine factors: excellent quality of tea leaves, fresh and clean water drawn from a spring or river known for its fine water, good tea ware, pleasing guests, and beautiful surroundings in which to drink the tea.

Proper Moments for Drinking Tea

When one's hearts and hands are idle.
Tired after reading poetry.
When one's thoughts are disturbed.
Listening to songs and ditties.
When a song is completed.
Shut up at one's home on a holiday.
Playing the *ch'in** and looking over paintings.
Engaged in conversation deep at night.
Before a bright window and a clean desk.
With charming friends and slender concubines.
Returning from a visit with friends.
When the day is clear and the breeze is mild.
On a day of light showers.
In a painted boat near a small wooden bridge.
In a forest with tall bamboos.
In a pavilion overlooking lotus flowers on a
summer day.
Having lighted incense in a small studio.
After a feast is over and the guests are gone.
When children are at school.
In a quiet, secluded temple.
Near famous springs and quaint rocks.

—Hsu Ts'eshu, *Ch'asu*

*Chinese stringed instrument.

Author's Note: Some of the readers of *The Tea Book* manuscript considered part of this poem sexist. I refer specifically to the mention of *slender concubines* (line 10). The poem is presented here because I wish to represent various cultures' views of tea.

MI GAO CHA (RICE-CAKE TEA)

This method of making tea has been in use for many centuries in China. It is still utilized in some parts of the country today. Boil rice cakes and powdered green tea together until the mixture is thick and syrupy. To make this tea less bitter tasting, add thin slices of ginger to the mixture as it is boiling. Serve.

TI-KUAN-YIN (IRON GODDESS OF MERCY TEA)

This is an Oolong tea, grown in the Wu-I mountains of Fukien and in Guangdong. The tea was probably named after the Temple of Kuan-Yin, situated close to where the tea gardens were planted.

A small pot, barely large enough to hold 4 half-cups, is one-third filled with loose tea leaves. Hot water is poured over the leaves. Because the quantity of tea leaves used is large, the tea is immediately poured into cups and drunk right away. The tea is very thick. When the pot is empty, the kettle is filled again with fresh water and put on the fire to prepare the second pot, where the same leaves will be re-infused.

Chinese tradition looks upon the second pot of tea as being the best. As one Chinese author commented, "The first pot is compared to a girl of thirteen, the second is compared to a girl of sweet sixteen, and the third is regarded as a woman."

PU-ERH CHA (TROUSER-SEAT TEA)

This tea grows wild in the southwestern part of China. *Pu-erh* tea got its name a long time ago when young girls picking it used to hide tea leaves in the seats of their wide trousers to sell to customers on the side. It can include green, Oolong, red, and white teas (see next page). It is sold in brick and loose form. Traditionally, this tea was boiled into a decoction.

These days, *Pu-erh* tea is more popular among the tribal peoples along the southwestern border of China and in Laos, Myanmar, and Thailand. It is considered medicinal, and is drunk as a "curing tea," a general tonic, and an energizer. It is also used to treat colds and sore throats. *Pu-erh* is exported and can be found in Chinese specialty stores throughout North America.

BAI YIE CHA (WHITE TEA)

These teas, which boast white leaves, are grown in the southwestern province of Yunnan. Although several varieties are available, this is not a popular tea for export or for drinking in China. According to historical documentation, white tea was far more abundant and popular during the Sung Dynasty.

PAO-CHUNG (PAPER-WRAPPED TEA)

This is a lightly fermented tea (12-15 percent fermentation, compared to the 40-60 percent of Oolongs). It is referred to as *pao-chung* because at one time the tea leaves were wrapped in paper before being fired.

ZHUAN CHA (BRICK TEA)

For centuries in China, tea was used as a form of money for bartering. It was steamed, pulverized, and compressed into brick form. Then calligraphy or a scene of a temple or landscape was stamped into the top surface of each brick.

Lu Yu in the *Ch'a Ching* mentions the early manufacturing of brick tea. "All there is to making tea is to pick it, steam it, pound it, shape it, dry it, tie it and seal it."

These days, brick teas are oblong bricks of tea usually made with the fannings, dust, stems, and twigs left over from other grades of tea. Some brick teas, however, are made from steamed and compressed tea leaves. Brick tea is usually a poorer-quality tea. More commonly used in northern Russia (Siberia) and Central Asia, this tea is not exported to the West.

JU HUA CHA (CHRYSANTHEMUM TEA)

Both black and green teas are scented with flower blossoms in China. Some of the more common petals used to scent teas are from the following flowering plants: chrysanthemum, jasmine, gardenia, lotus, orange, plum, and rose. Flower-blossom teas are drunk mainly in northern China.

Drunk since the Sung Dynasty, chrysanthemum tea was thought to help prevent illnesses, such as colds and viral infections. As a relaxant, it was also considered useful in relieving headaches.

Chrysanthemum tea can be made as a straight infusion of the dried petals of this flower, or the petals can be added to tea leaves while they are steeping. Dried blossom powders are also available and are utilized in the same way as blossoms.

The Chinese people love chrysanthemums and hundreds of varieties are grown for decoration. Only one variety, however, the sweet chrysanthemum, is grown for tea. The very best is grown near Hangchow.

Chrysanthemum tea may be purchased at Chinese specialty stores. Follow the directions on the packaging for infusing. Sweeten the tea with sugar, if preferred.

SHIANG PIAN CHA (JASMINE TEA)

Jasmine grows in abundance in southern China. Jasmine tea is probably the most widely exported of any of the Chinese flower-scented teas. The flowers are used to scent both green and manufactured "red" (black) teas.

To scent green tea, fully fired green tea leaves and jasmine flowers are placed in wicker baskets in alternating two-inch layers. The flowers are dried in the baskets for a day and then removed.

To manufacture jasmine-scented red tea, the jasmine petals are dried and powdered. This powder is mixed with the black tea leaves during the last phase of drying. Jasmine teas are usually infused for the same length of time as are black teas.

When making jasmine tea, follow the directions given on the packaging.

JU ZI HUA CHA (ORANGE-BLOSSOM TEA)

Orange-blossom tea is made by blending equal portions of fragrant orange-blossom petals with green tea leaves. Place dried petals and green tea in a pot. Pour boiling water over the blend and infuse. This is a highly fragrant tea.

MEI GUI CHA (ROSE-BLOSSOM TEA)

Rose-blossom tea is tea leaves blended with rose petals. Add rose petals to green or black tea leaves in a teapot. Pour boiling water over the blend and infuse it for 5 minutes or until the tea is the strength you desire.

In 1618, tea (*tchai*) arrived in Russia from Mongolia. Early imported tea was crushed into powdered form and steamed into bricks to facilitate transport. The bricks were packed into little boxes and carried 11,000 miles across Manchuria by camel tea caravans. A single journey took about sixteen months. The major tea-caravan years were from 1860 to 1880, ending when the Trans-Siberian railway became the major transportation link.

Today, Russians drink black tea that is imported from India or Sri Lanka. Tea is also grown in Georgia and Azerbaijan.

RUSSKY TCHAI (RUSSIAN TEA)

Russian Tea is a combination of *zavarka* (strong tea essence) and samovar-heated water. A samovar, which means "self-cooker," is a large urn that heats and holds hot water for tea. It often has a metal holder on top of it to secure a teapot filled with zavarka. In the center of the samovar is a wide hollow tube that holds hot charcoals. The charcoals heat the water surrounding the tube.

Russian samovars have been embellished over the years. They have been made from silver and brass complete with engraved or relief designs.

The first thing a Russian does in the morning after waking is to start up the samovar to make tea. The samovar is kept going all day, maintaining a ready supply of hot water. Russians often drink tea all day long and guests are customarily offered a cup when they come calling. Although electric samovars are readily available today, many people do not think of these electric urns as "real" samovars. To create your own version of a samovar, *see* "Iran."

Zavarka is a concentrated tea essence made from tea leaves and hot water. Russians believe only a ceramic or porcelain teapot should be used to make zavarka because a metalic pot will affect the taste of the tea. To make zavarka, fill a small porcelain teapot with 1 tsp. of loose tea leaves per 6 oz. hot water. For an even stronger zavarka, use 1 tsp. of tea leaves per 3 oz. hot water.

Add samovar-heated hot water to the teapot. Set the teapot with the zavarka on top of the warm samovar. Infuse the tea leaves for 10 minutes. The zavarka will stay heated on top of the samovar.

Russian Tea is made by filling a cup about one-quarter full with zavarka. Preheated hot water from the samovar is then added to fill the cup.

An electric samovar.

A Russian porcelain teacup with lid.

This tea has a slight bitter taste, as is preferred by most tea-drinking Russians.

PIT' TCHAI PO KUSKY (SUGAR CUBES WITH TEA)

Russians love to drink their tea with sugar. Sugar dissolved in tea is believed to enhance the flavor of the leaves. A favorite method of drinking tea is to place a sugar cube between one's teeth and sip the hot tea through the cube.

TCHAI S LEMONOM (TEA WITH LEMON)

It is believed that it was the Russians who first began the widespread practice of serving tea with a "twist of lemon peel" or a lemon wedge. Queen Victoria of England experienced this custom when she visited the Russian court, and took the idea back to England with her.

In recent years fresh lemons have been hard to come by in Russia. Russians still leave *tchai s lemonom* written on their restaurant menus, reflecting their sensitivity to the hard times that have deprived them of their beloved citrus-flavored tea drink.

Try adding the twist of lemon to Georgian or Russian Caravan Tea. It should be noted, however, that "Russian Caravan Tea" is not tea from Russia. It is a blend of Chinese and Indian teas often associated with the import of teas to Russia during the caravan years.

TCHAI S OSENNIM YABLOKOM (AUTUMN APPLE TEA)

1 cup hot brewed tea
Raw honey or sugar to taste
1 apple, peeled and chopped into small pieces

Fill a tea glass three-quarters full with hot tea. Sweeten the tea with sugar or honey and add the apple pieces. Let stand several minutes, then eat the apple pieces with a spoon and drink the tea. This is a favorite autumn-time tea in Russia. Serves 1.

TCHAI S YABLOKOM (APPLE TEA)

Float a slice of apple on top of the tea in each glass.

TCHAI S VARENYEM
(TEA WITH JAM OR PRESERVES)

The Russian aristocracy of the tea-caravan era served preserves with their tea, and Russians are still famous for their fruit tea. Russian women keep their pantries as well stocked as possible with preserves. The preserves are made so that the fruit holds its shape, surrounded by a thick, clear syrup.

A good hostess will always have two or three different homemade preserves on hand to serve with tea. Russians like their tea sweet, so if lots of sugar isn't added to tea, preserves are the ideal substitute. They add a delicate fruit flavor as well.

Each preserve is served on a small, flat, cut-glass or crystal jam dish called a *rozetki*. The drinker spoons the preserve into the teacup. The drinker can also eat the jam directly from the plate, and follow up or "chase" it with a sip of hot tea. Tea with jam is excellent as an accompaniment to a breakfast of Russian *blini,* filled pancakes.

TCHAI S MALINAVOYE VARENYEM
(RASPBERRY JAM TEA)

Russians believe that if you drink tea with raspberry jam, it will ward off colds. To each glass of hot tea, add 1 tsp. of raspberry jam.

TCHAI S VODKOI (VODKA TEA)

Vodka is a clear strong spirit produced from the starch or sugar of potatoes, grapes, corn, rye, wheat, or molasses. The name is derived from *zhizenennia voda,* which means "water of life." Russian production of vodka began in the thirteenth century at the Fort of Viataka.

After work or in the evenings, Russians may relax with tea spiked with vodka. To each glass of tea, add desired amount of vodka.

TCHAINAYA (TEA-FLAVORED VODKA)

4 tsp. black tea leaves
2 cups charcoal-filtered vodka

Take a clean pint jar and place the tea leaves in the bottom. Fill the jar with vodka. Seal tightly and give it a shake for a few seconds. Store at room temperature. After 24 hours, filter the tea-flavored vodka through a sieve.

Add to hot tea in desired amounts or drink by itself. Sip *tchainaya* slowly.

A lighter *tchainaya* may be preferred. Make it by using 1 tsp. tea leaves and 1 cup vodka.

PLITOCHNYI TCHAI (BRICK TEA)

The leaves, stems, and twigs of green and black teas are used to make brick teas. Most often, brick tea is made from the lowest grades of tea. The tea particles are steamed until they are pliable, then packed into wooden brick-shaped molds and stored until they have dried hard.

This "last of the lot," poor-grade tea is given to those people considered "the last of the lot" in Russia—the Siberian exiles. Male exiles are usually placed eight prisoners to a cell. Each day they gather to brew tea. The tea is placed in a metal cup of water. Pieces of paper or other flammable materials are lit on fire and the prisoners hold the flammables under the cup(s) to heat the tea.

During the caravan era, the Russians bartered with brick tea. Bricks of tea with picturesque scenes stamped on them were used for purchasing goods.

During times of a tea surplus in Russia, tea bricks have been used for fuel. So, not only would one drink tea for warmth, but the surplus fueled a fire on a cold winter's night.

TCHAI S KOSLINYM MOLOKOM Y HLEBOM (GOAT'S MILK AND BREAD TEA)

To make this tea recipe from Turkestan, boil tea leaves in water in a thin copper pot until the tea is dark in color and strong in taste. Add goat's milk cream to the hot tea. Allow the tea leaves to settle. Turkestan tea is "eaten," so to speak, by dipping pieces of bread into it.

Goat's milk cream may be difficult to obtain. Substitute plain goat's milk if you cannot find the cream in a specialty store.

THE CZECH REPUBLIC AND SLOVAKIA

Tea is not drunk very often in the Czech Republic or Slovakia. For most of the people in these two countries, coffee is the daily drink of choice. Tea is available, however, in shops and tearooms, which serve a choice of the beverage and pastries. It is also served at bistros or cafés. During the day the bistros are occupied by local men playing chess and chatting up the day as they sip endless cups of coffee or tea.

Tea can be served in cups or glasses. Since the glasses are hot to touch, one has to learn how to hold them between the fingers.

Only black tea is drunk in the Czech Republic and Slovakia. It is imported from Georgia in the C.I.S. as well as from Sri Lanka. Jasmine tea from China is also available.

In the Czech Republic and Slovakia, tea is made in the usual way by pouring boiling water over loose black tea in a *chaoua konice* (teapot) and steeping. The tea is ready to be served when the tea leaves have settled.

When ordering tea in a café, one would ask for:

Cha: black tea.
Cha s mlekem: tea with milk.
Cha s citronem: tea with lemon.

DENMARK

Breakfast in Denmark can be coffee and bread or tea plus a hard-boiled egg. The latter is popularly known as *en te complet*. To request tea in Denmark, ask for:

En kop sort te: a cup of tea.
Te med fløde: tea with cream.
Te med sukker: tea with sugar.

Tea is made in Denmark by steeping a tea bag in boiling water for a few minutes.

EGYPT

Tea drinking began in Egypt in the fifteenth century. As a rule, Eyptians like to drink their tea sweet.

CHAI BIL YANSOON (ANISEED TEA)

Anise, native to western Asia and Egypt, has something of a licorice taste. Add a few aniseeds to tea leaves in a teapot. Pour in boiling water and steep the mixture for 5 minutes. Strain aniseed-flavored tea into cups. Sweeten with sugar if desired. This tea is delicious hot, cold, or iced.

ENGLAND

In 1658, tea was first served and sold publicly at Thomas Garway's Coffee House in Exchange Alley, London. Coffeehouses were the social gathering places of the time and coffee was a popular drink in the country. The English came to prefer the simpler method of making tea to the longer time it took to brew coffee.

The English prefer their tea white or brown colored (with milk). In the early days of tea drinking in England, the porcelain ware was fragile and would crack easily, so milk was added to the cups first to decrease the trauma to the ware caused by the temperature of the hot tea. Tea tasters for the English tea market add milk to the sample infusions before testing for the quality of teas, because that is how most of the English will prepare their tea.

Tea in England can be served straight (without sugar or milk), white (with milk), or white with sugar (milk and sugar). It is made with tea bags, which were introduced to the British public in 1953. Interestingly, when the tea bag was first introduced, many British people were suspicious of it. It was thought that hidden within the confines of the bag was an inferior tea. The tea bag did catch on and early tea-bag tea was made by throwing another tea bag into the teapot along with the old one and adding more hot water. When the teapot was cleaned at the end of the day, a handful of tea bags would have to be removed from it.

While the English believe "only in England can the best cuppa tea be had" (see "Tea Brewing Methods—Steeping or Infusion"), the irony of all of this is that their early suspicions were accurate. The tea bag in comparison to larger tea leaves does

A Davenport boat-shaped teapot of the early nineteenth century.

A Grainger (Worcester) teapot ca. 1825-30.

produce an inferior cup. With 85 percent of the English public utilizing tea bags, this is not something they want to hear! They insist, however, that they only import the best-grade leaves for their tea bags.

AN EARLY JESUIT RECIPE

The walnut shell was used for many years in England to measure tea leaves for the pot. Use a walnut shell to measure the amount of tea you put into your teapot. Pour boiling water over the leaves and steep. Traditionally it was suggested by the Jesuit priests that the steeping time of tea leaves was equal to the time it took for a person to read the Penitent's Psalm (Psalm 51).

EGG TEA I

In the late 1800s and early 1900s an English tea-drinking trend was to serve a well-beaten, frothy raw egg in tea as a substitute for milk. To make Egg Tea, beat 1 egg in a bowl until it is liquefied and bubbly. Pour the egg liquid into the bottom of a teacup. Fill the rest of the cup with hot tea, stirring constantly with a spoon as you slowly add it. Serves 1.

EGG TEA II

This is another old English recipe. Place an egg yolk and fine sugar (to taste) in a bowl. Whip the ingredients with a spoon or a fork until they are well mixed together. Place the yolk-sugar mixture in a teacup and fill the cup with hot tea. Serves 1.

CAMBRIC TEA

England's version of Cambric Tea is light and milky (see "France"). Sometimes referred to as "Nursery Tea," this tea is served by nurseries to children in midmorning and midafternoon to help sustain them through their energetic days. For generations, Cambric Tea has also been Mama's choice for her young children when they sit with her at teatime.

1 cup milk
1 tsp. strong tea
Sugar to taste

Heat milk. Add the strong tea infusion to the hot milk. Add sugar to taste. Serves 1.

The amounts of milk and tea essence used in Cambric Tea may be adjusted to suit personal tastes.

VANILLA NURSERY TEA

To make a variation of Cambric Tea, stir in ½ tsp. of vanilla extract for each cup of milk as it is being heated.

ICED MILK TEA

Make tea in the usual way, but infuse the tea leaves in scalding milk instead of boiling water. Sweeten tea with sugar to taste then strain into a pitcher. Chill the milk tea in a refrigerator before serving.

ORANGE SPICED TEA

Place 4 tsp. Orange Pekoe-grade tea leaves, a few cut-up cloves, and one or more strips of dried orange peel (pith removed) in a pot. Pour 3 cups boiling water over and steep for 5 minutes. Strain through cup strainers into cups. Serves 4.

ORANGE ORCHARD TEA

Fill teacups one-third full with freshly squeezed orange juice. Fill the remainder of each cup with tea. Serve with an orange wedge or float a thin, almost transparent slice of orange on top of each tea drink.

Note: Traditionally, teacups are not filled to the brim, but to three-quarters full to avoid spills.

APPLE ORCHARD TEA

Fill teacups one-third full with hot apple juice. Fill remainder of each cup with hot tea. Float a peeled slice of apple on top.

LEMON-TREE TEA

To hot tea, add Lemon Syrup (see "Tea Syrups" chapter) to taste. Serve each tea with a twist of lemon. Or serve hot tea with lemon wedges on the side. Squeeze desired amount of lemon juice into tea. Add sugar to sweeten, if desired.

TEA WITH A TWIST

Queen Victoria introduced Tea with a Twist (tea with lemon slice, wedge, or peel) to the English. The lemon juice or peel is added to the tea to give it a slight lemony taste and fragrance. Queen Victoria learned this Russian tea custom when she was visiting her eldest daughter, the Princess Royal, at the Russian court.

LEMON-SCENTED TEA

To the bottom of a canister, add a few pieces of lemon peel. (Make sure the white pith is removed.) Fill canister with tea leaves. After a short period, the lemon peel will scent the tea.

PEACH-SCENTED TEA

Add a few drops of peach oil to the tea leaves stored in a tea caddy.

CLOVE AND ORANGE-SCENTED TEA

Place cloves (freshly cut in half to release vapors) and dried orange-peel strips (with the white pith scraped away) in the bottom of your tea caddy. Fill with Ceylon tea leaves. Seal caddy with a tight lid and let leaves and spices sit for a few days. The tea will then be scented and ready for use.

VANILLA-SCENTED TEA

Add a few drops of vanilla extract to a few tea leaves. Let the vanilla-treated tea leaves dry. Then add these scented tea leaves to a tea caddy filled with tea leaves. Or, add 2 vanilla pods to a tea caddy filled with tea leaves.

CINNAMON-SCENTED TEA

Add a few cinnamon sticks to the tea leaves stored in a tea caddy. The cinnamon sticks may be removed before steeping the leaves, or may infuse along with them.

ROSE-PETAL TEA

In creating your own blossom teas, experiment by adding different kinds of flower blossoms in varying amounts to loose green or black tea leaves. Flower teas purvey unique tastes with wonderful fragrances.

For each cup of loose black tea leaves, add ¼ cup dried rose petals. Store the mixture in a tea caddy with a tight seal.

To make tea, steep 1 tsp. of rose-petal tea mixture in 6 oz. of boiling water for 5 minutes. Serves 1.

ROSE-PETAL-JASMINE TEA

For each cup of Chinese jasmine tea leaves, add ¼ cup dried rose petals. Store the mixture in a tea caddy with a tight seal.

To make tea, steep 1 tsp. of rose-petal-jasmine tea mixture in 6 oz. of boiling water for 5 minutes. Serves 1.

ENGLISH LAVENDER TEA

To each cup of tea leaves, add 4 tsp. dried English lavender flowers. Store the mixture in a seal-tight tea caddy. Blossoms can become stale much quicker than tea leaves, so use this tea within weeks after blending.

To make tea, infuse 1 tsp. of lavender tea blend in 6 oz. of boiling water for 5 minutes. Strain tea into a teacup. Serves 1.

ETHIOPIA

Ethiopia grows tea for its own local use. It also imports tea from Sri Lanka. Although Ethiopia is primarily a coffee-producing and coffee-drinking country, tea is drunk by almost all Ethiopians, children included. Tea drinking begins at an early age; babies are given their first slurps of it from baby bottles. The favorite time for drinking tea in Ethiopia is at breakfast, where it is accompanied by bread.

Tea can be drunk any time throughout the day depending on the drinker's preference. It can be purchased in restaurants or in *shay baatoch,* tea shops. Popular snacking accompaniments are chunks of spicy, whole-wheat bread or fried, doughnutlike pastries.

Loose tea for home consumption is purchased in various quantities at *sookoch,* market shops. When making tea in Ethiopia, water is boiled in a kettle or a pot on a charcoal stove. Black tea leaves are added to the kettle and the tea is steeped for about 5 minutes. A straight infusion is poured off the top of the pot into *birchikoch,* 6-oz. glasses. A cup strainer may also be used.

BERRAD (SPICY TEA)

Berrad is made in a small, aluminum teapot called a berrad *or a* berrad-pot, *although well-established restaurants have berrad-pots made of porcelain. The berrad-pot usually makes about three to four little cups (cinneoch) of tea. In Ethiopia, berrad is drunk along with the chewing of the herb khat. Khat, a plant known for its narcotic qualities, is used as a social substance in Ethiopia when people gather in small groups to chat and spend some fun time together. Some Ethiopians chew khat and drink berrad to help them relax after a long day's work.*

**3 cardamom pods, crushed with the round edge
   of a spoon
3 cloves, cut in half
A few "tiny" pieces of cinnamon stick
   (to equal about ⅛-in. stick)
2 tsp. black tea leaves
1½ cups boiling water**

Place dry ingredients in a small teapot. Fill with water. Cover and let the tea and the spices steep for about 5 minutes. Strain the tea into little cups. Serves 3-4.

In 1657, Cardinal Mazarin and French surgeon Pierre Cressy publicly proclaimed *le thé* a cure for gout. For the next thirty or forty years, tea drinking remained popular in France, but soon thereafter the French became enamored with coffee. France remains a coffee-drinking nation.

THE NOIR (BLACK TEA)

Thé noir, a straight infusion, may be drunk at breakfast and at five o'clock, which is considered the "teatime" in France.

THE AU LAIT (TEA WITH MILK)

A bowl of café au lait is a commonly enjoyed breakfast drink in France. However, some people prefer a bowl of thé au lait instead, served with their continental breakfast of croissants and jam.

1 cup scalded milk
1 cup hot tea
Sugar to taste

Mix equal amounts of scalding hot milk and tea together in a bowl, pouring the two liquids into the bowl at the same time. Sweeten with sugar. Serves 1-2.

THE DE CAMBRAI (CAMBRIC TEA)

This white-colored tea was named after the white Cambric linen fabric that originated in the city of Cambrai in France. The English and the French each have slightly different versions of Cambric Tea. The English version uses milk instead of cream. For both nationalities, this is a "white tea," meant to be served as a nutritious drink. It is given to children, to the sick, or to anyone wishing to partake of a warm drink without having to experience the stimulating effects of tea.

Sugar to taste (suggest 1 tsp. per cup)
Heavy cream
Boiling water
Hot tea, strongly brewed

Put sugar in a cup. Fill the cup to one-third full with rich, heavy cream. Stir the cream and the sugar until the sugar dissolves. Then fill the cup with boiling water. Add a couple of tablespoons of strongly brewed tea to give it a light tea taste. Serves 1.

GERMANY

The Germans are mainly coffee drinkers, having never developed a taste for tea. Black tea, however, is available for those who prefer it. It is drunk *mit Milch* (with milk) or *mit Zitrone* (with lemon). Tea in Germany is made and served the same way as in England. Russian-style tea glasses set in filigreed metal holders are also available.

Tea may be purchased at *Gasthauses* (guesthouses), inns, and *Kaffeehauses* (coffeehouses). Sweet desserts are served along with it. Some of the most common accompaniments are: *Apfel Strudel* (apple strudel), *Schwarz-Walder Kirsche* (blackforest cake), *Schokoladen Kuchen* (chocolate cake), and *Haselnuss Torte* (hazelnut cake).

OST FRIESISCHER TEE (EAST FRISIAN TEA)

Surprisingly, there is one area of Germany that is predominantly tea drinking—East Frisia on the North Sea. About three-quarters of the tea imported to Germany is consumed in this area. East Frisians drink tea throughout the day, and have scheduled teatimes or tea breaks in the morning and afternoon.

East Frisians sweeten their tea by placing rock sugar in the bottom of their cups. The large rocks sometimes take up as much as one-third of the teacup space. The sugar does not dissolve in the first cup of tea. A second or a third cup is required to dispense with it.

Nevertheless, East Frisians prefer a bitter-tasting tea. This is made by the usual steeping method, but extra tea leaves are added to the teapot to produce a stronger infusion. The tea is also steeped for longer than usual.

Lastly, and most notably, East Frisians drink their tea in layers. They top the tea with a layer of cream that has been spooned off the top of their milk. Tea is drunk cream first, bitter brew second, and sweetened sugar tea, at the bottom of the cup, last.

HONG KONG

CHA

The people of Hong Kong drink green teas and Oolong teas, made the same way as tea is made in China. Green tea leaves are imported to Hong Kong from mainland China and Oolong tea leaves are imported from Taiwan.

INDIA, PAKISTAN, AND BANGLADESH

The people of India like their black tea milky and sweet. *Chai* is served at *dhabas* or *chai dukans,* small tea-serving establishments found everywhere in India. Even in the countryside, a *chai dukan* can be found almost in the middle of nowhere. Farmers have built thatched-roofed, open-air *dukans* by roads near their fields to have tea in and to relax away from the hot sun. Open fireplaces are built outdoors beside the huts.

I remember an experience in northern India in 1972 while travelling by van up the long lonely highway to Nepal. The van broke down in the middle of nowhere—but not too far from a farmer's *chai dukan.* My friend (coauthor of *The Coffee Book*) and I spent a blistering, sun-filled day relaxing on woven rattan cots under the shade of the thatched *dukan,* drinking glassful after glassful of sweet tea. The van owner, on the other hand, spent the entire day travelling north or south (which way—I cannot remember) searching for automobile parts.

HINDUSTANI CHAI #1 (INDIAN TEA)

6 oz. water
2 tsp. black tea leaves
2-4 tsp. sugar
6 oz. boiling milk

Bring water, tea leaves, and sugar to a boil in a pot. Add boiling milk. Turn down the heat, cover the pot, and allow the mixture to simmer for 5 minutes. Strain the mixture through a sieve into metal cups or glass tumblers. Serves 2.

Note: Pasteurized milk is not readily available in the rural areas of India, so milk must be boiled. Tea may be sweetened with cane sugar, beet sugar, or palm sugar. Palm sugar called *jaggery* is made from the sap of various palms.

HINDUSTANI CHAI #2

1 cup water
2 tea bags or 2 tsp. loose tea leaves
Sugar to taste
½ cup milk

Bring water, tea bags or leaves, and sugar to a boil in a pot. Add milk and simmer for 5 minutes. If loose tea has been used, strain the mixture through a sieve into plastic tumblers. Serves 2. This recipe may be doubled or tripled.

HINDUSTANI CHAI #3

Make a strong tea infusion with tea leaves and boiling water. Fill a plastic tumbler to one-quarter full with boiling milk. Then fill with the tea. Add sugar to taste. Serves 1.

SINGHPO CHAI (TEA OF THE SINGHPOS)

In the Assam region of northeastern India, long before the English began cultivating tea in the area, the Singhpos (native hill tribes of the Assam jungle) used the wild tea plant, native to the jungle, to make a souplike drink. Their "tea-soup," called *miang,* is similar to the fermented tea made by the Shan tribes of northern Thailand and Myanmar (formerly Burma).

To ferment the tea leaves, the Singhpos dug a hole in the earth and lined it with large leaves. The tea leaves were boiled, the liquid disposed of, and the wet tea leaves put into the hole in the ground. The wet tea leaves were then covered with tree leaves and dirt, and allowed to ferment for several weeks. After the tea leaves were removed, they were mixed with oil and garlic.

NIMBU-ELACHI CHAI (LEMON-CARDAMOM TEA)

It is believed the lemon tree is native to northern India. Both the lemon fruit and its peel are used for culinary flavoring and in fruit drinks. The cardamom plant is indigenous to southern India, growing in Mysore and Madras.

5-6 green cardamom pods
2¼ cups water
3 tsp. black tea leaves
A few thin strips lemon peel
Boiled milk
Sugar to taste

Bring the cardamom pods and water to a boil. Add the tea leaves and the lemon-peel strips. Turn down heat, cover pot, and simmer all of the ingredients for a few minutes. Strain the tea into glasses. Serve with hot milk and sugar. Serves 3.

MASALI WALI CHAI #1 (SPICED TEA)

4 tsp. tea leaves
A few cloves
A few cardamom pods, crushed
A few thin strips lemon peel
3 cups boiling water
Boiled milk
Sugar to taste

Place tea leaves and spices in a pot. Add water and steep the mixture for 5 minutes. Pour a small amount of boiled milk into each cup. Strain the tea through a metal sieve into the cups. Sweeten the tea with sugar. Serves 4.

MASALI WALI CHAI #2

1 cup milk
1 clove
1 cinnamon stick (3 in.)
1 heaping tsp. sugar
1 cardamom pod, crushed
1 tsp. tea leaves

Place all of the ingredients except the tea leaves in a pot. Heat the mixture to a boil, add tea leaves, and continue boiling the mixture for another 2 minutes. Remove the tea from the heat and allow it to steep for 3 minutes. Strain the tea into glasses. More sugar may be added to taste. This recipe may be doubled or tripled.

SAUNF WALI CHAI (ANISEED TEA)

Anise is one of the most ancient spices known to man. Originally it was cultivated by the Egyptians. Today, it is widely cultivated in India. In ancient folklore, aniseed was considered an aphrodisiac. These days, it is regarded mainly as a culinary spice, although it has some carminative value.

¼ tsp. aniseeds (more optional)
1 cup water
1 cup brewed black tea (Darjeeling/Assam)
Sugar to taste
Scalded or boiled milk (optional)

Boil the aniseeds in water in a covered pot. When the aniseeds are soft, strain the liquid. Mix brewed tea and aniseed liquid.
Add sugar. Scalded or boiled milk may be added if desired. Serves 2.

SAUNF WALI THANDI CHAI
(ICED ANISEED TEA)

Aniseed tea tastes nice served cold or iced. Cool the aniseed tea (see previous recipe) for a few hours. Pour the cooled tea into glasses, over ice. Serves 2.

YOGI CHAI (YOGI TEA)

There are numerous variations of India spiced teas. Here is the variation known as Yogi Tea, introduced to Western countries by Sri Singh Harbhajan Singh Kalsa Yogi Ji. This is a stronger-tasting spice tea because of the addition of peppercorns.

4 cups hot water
18 whole cloves
2 cinnamon sticks
18 green cardamom pods
18 black peppercorns
4 thin slices gingerroot or a 1-in. piece
    of crystallized ginger
4 tsp. black tea leaves
4 cups milk
Sugar to taste

Lightly boil water and spices in a covered pot for 20 minutes. Reduce the heat and add tea leaves. Steep for a few minutes. About 3 cups of liquid will remain.

In a separate pot, heat milk to boiling point. Filter the tea through a metal sieve into glasses, filling each glass one-third to one-half full. Fill the rest of each glass with the boiling milk. Stir. Sweeten with sugar if desired. Serves 8. This recipe may be halved.

INDONESIA

Tea is grown in many parts of Indonesia, the country being an archipelago of over thirteen thousand islands. The most well known of the teas exported from Indonesia are grown in West Java and Sumatra. The best-quality teas are shipped to Japan, North America, and Western Europe, where they are usually used in blends. Black tea is also imported from India and Sri Lanka.

Although Indonesia is a tea-producing nation, it does not as yet boast tea specialty shops. Tea is purchased from grocery stores in quantities of loose leaves or in prewrapped, paper packages. The poorer grades are utilized by the Indonesians. The better grades are only available in special shops for those who can afford them. Tea bags are available, but those too are usually only purchased by the elite.

Some Indonesians grow their own tea on family plots and on farms in and around villages. If freshly picked tea leaves are being used to make tea, the leaves are first laid out to dry in the sun. After sun drying, the leaves are dry fry heated in an iron pan on a wood stove.

In many restaurants in Indonesia, tea is served automatically to customers without charge. The quality of drinking water is poor in some parts of the country, so tea is utilized to disguise the smell and color of the water. Tea is drunk from porcelain teacups. Tin cups that are manufactured in Indonesia are commonly used in villages. In busy public areas such as bus terminals and train stations, *teh es,* iced tea, can be obtained from vendors. It is served in small plastic bags drawn tight around the rim with elastic bands. A straw is inserted through the elastic into the bag.

To request *teh* in Indonesia, ask for:

Teh pahit: tea without sugar.
Teh manis: tea with sugar.
Teh susu: tea with milk; sweetened condensed milk is added.
Teh es: iced tea, sweetened with sugar.

INDUK TEH (MOTHER TEA)

This tea is so named to symbolize the strong and central role the mother has in the family. Teko (teapots) are sometimes used in Indonesian homes; however, it is more common for a tea essence to be prepared ahead of time and then used when desired. The tea essence is made in large cups, then transferred in desired amounts to drinking cups. Boiling water is added to the tea essence in each cup. Even in large restaurants in Indonesia, a tea essence is made up in larger containers. The essence is used throughout the day, whenever tea is ordered. Elderly people in Indonesia generally prefer to drink a strong brew. A very strong tea is also given as a treatment for diarrhea.

Fill an 8-oz. cup to one-quarter full with loose black tea leaves. Then fill the cup to three-quarters full with boiling water. Infuse the tea leaves for 2 minutes, stirring constantly. Wait until the tea leaves settle, then pour the desired portion of tea essence into each person's cup. Add boiling water to the cups. Each person will determine the strength of the brew. Cold milk, sugar and milk, or just sugar may be added depending on personal preference. Pasteurized milk is available in Indonesia;

however, most people prefer to use sweetened condensed milk or powdered milk in their tea. White granulated sugar is the desired sweetener even though Indonesia has its own sugarcane plantations.

Tea strainers are not normally used in Indonesia. If there are too many tea leaves floating in a cup, they are removed with a spoon. Most Indonesians do not mind a few leaves in their tea.

TEH TELUR (TEA WITH EGG)

In Indonesia, Teh Telur is drunk for its taste and as an "energizer."

Crack a raw egg into the bottom of a large cup. Whip the egg until completely liquified. (This tea can also be made with just the yolk.) Fill the cup three-quarters full with boiling water, stirring constantly. Add a desired amount of tea essence (see Induk Teh). Sweeten with sugar to taste. Serves 1.

IRAN

Tea grows in tea gardens in northern Iran from the Elburtz Mountains to the Caspian Sea. It is cultivated for domestic use. Tea is also imported to Iran from Sri Lanka.

Tea drinking is a much cherished tradition in Iran. Like the Russians, Iranians heat up a samovar first thing in the morning and keep it hot all day for endless cups of *cha-yi.* Breakfast includes tea with bread and cheese.

Tea is served in small glasses without handles called *estekanha,* or it is sipped from saucers. One can obtain *cha-yi* in teahouses *(chaikhang-ie)* anywhere in Iran. Beautiful Persian rugs cover the floors for visitors and locals to squat on while drinking. Benches with cushions often line the four walls. In the rural areas, teahouses are partitioned by a screen separating men from women. Many teahouses are frequented by men who gather to tell stories, listen to the radio, or chat.

When tea is served at home, the eldest woman in the family is bestowed the honor of serving the tea.

CHA-YI (BREWED TEA)

1 heaping tsp. tea leaves
6 oz. boiling water

Place tea leaves in a teapot. Cover the tea leaves with water. Place the teapot on top of your "homemade samovar."

To simulate your own substitute samovar: Fill a large pot with water. Cover with a flat lid and set on stove. Bring the water to a boil. Then lower heat and let the water simmer. Place the teapot with the tea essence in it on top of the "samovar" lid. The tea essence will stay warm on top of the pot for a long time.

To make tea: Fill a small glass one-third full with the tea essence. Then fill the rest of the glass with hot water from your homemade samovar.

CHA-YI ALKH

Tea is bitter tasting in Iran. If the tea is to be sweetened, a sugar cube is dipped in the tea and then placed under one's tongue. Tea in Iran is drunk without milk.

CHA-YI SHEEREEN

Add lots of sugar to the *estekan* (tea glass) before sipping the tea.

IRAQ

Tea arrived in Iraq from Persia. Iraqi tea is made with a samovar and a tea essence. Tea is drunk straight, without milk or sugar, although sometimes a sugar lump is placed under one's tongue or between one's teeth, while the tea is being sipped.

Like its neighbors in the Middle East—Kuwait, Qatar, and Egypt—Iraq ranks among the top tea consumers in the world.

CHAI BIL YANSOON (ANISE TEA)

Add ½ tsp. of powdered aniseeds or 1 tsp. of aniseeds to the teapot when steeping a strong tea essence to be used with the samovar (see "Iran").

CHAI BI WARDET AL BERTAKAAN (ORANGE-BLOSSOM TEA)

The Seville orange is a bitter-tasting orange first known to the Greeks in the twelfth century. Orange drops made from the blossoms can be added to tea or to other foods as a flavoring.

IRELAND

Everyone has heard of the Irish's great love for tea. What is not widely known is that these days the Irish outstrip their English counterparts in the number of cups a day each person downs. The "cup o' tay" in Ireland is considered "the curer" and "the soother" for all ills. For example, if someone dies, the response to the mourners is "Have a cup of tay." If a person is injured, the usual reaction is "Have a cup of tay." If someone has a cold, the prescription is "Have a cup of tay." If a cat crosses one's path, the consolation given is "Have a cup of tay."

Tea is made both with loose leaves and with bags, although more commonly with the latter. It is a bitter-tasting, strong brew prepared by throwing more tea bags in a pot than one can shake a stick at and by steeping the brew for an excessively long period of time. Once the tea water has been heated in the kettle, it is poured into a pot or a teapot, which is set on a stove burner (low heat) for a minimum of 10 minutes. And that is a minimum! Sometimes the pot of tea is kept on the heat for hours at a time.

Whole milk can be added to the tea. To offset the brew's bitterness, spoonfuls and spoonfuls of sugar are added. Tea is drunk at breakfast and throughout the day. Favorite accompaniments are Guinness fruitcakes, cream cakes, and, of course, Irish soda bread with jam.

ISRAEL

Tea is the national drink of this multicultured country. Since Israel's independence in 1948, there has been a continual immigration by Jewish people from all over the world. These newcomers have brought with them their tea-drinking customs from a multitude of regions. Traditional Russian brewing preferences such as zavarka and the use of the samovar contrast here with the ancient customs of Israel's many Arab residents, who share their tea-making etiquette with that of their Middle Eastern neighbors such as the Syrians and the Lebanese. Meanwhile, the tea bag steeped in the teapot remains the favorite drink of thousands of tourists who visit the Holy Land each year.

Needless to say, tea drinking is a national Israeli pastime. It is particularly evident at the many sidewalk cafés that line the streets of cities like Tel Aviv and Jerusalem. Here Israelis "hang out" in large numbers socializing and relaxing.

When ordering tea in Israel, one might ask for:

Tay mit limehneh: tea with a twist of lemon.
Tay mit milkh: tea with milk.
Tay mit shmahnt: tea with cream.
Tay mit sokar: tea with sugar.

JAPAN

In Japan, you hear people call tea "Ocha." *Cha,* which means tea, has an *O* placed before it to signify "that which is honored." *Cha* is grown in Uji (Kyoto Prefecture), Shizuoka (Shizuoka Prefecture), and Ureshino and Yame (Kyushu Island District).

Beginning at the end of April or the first of May each year, many Japanese travel to the tea estates in Shizuoka to observe the first leaf growth (flush) of the tea plants. The Japanese refer to this first leaf growth in the spring as "the first cha" or "wakabi." Later in June, the leaves will spurt again. This is "the second cha."

On almost every urban street in Japan, there are vending machines. To the foreigner, this place seems to be the land of the vending machine: hot and cold drinks can be purchased from these machines, and the selection includes black teas. These are dispensed hot or cold and usually sweet depending on the push button the purchaser selects.

Petty street crime is statistically low in Japan, so the locals can enjoy this convenience without concern about the vending machines being broken into or damaged. Interestingly, despite so much usage, the machines seem to be kept in good repair. The author does not remember a single instance of a vending machine "drinking" her money when she visited Japan.

BANCHA (DRY-ROASTED TEA)

This is the everyday drink of the Japanese people, adults and children alike. Bancha is served at most restaurants in Japan. As soon as customers are seated, a teapot of bancha is brought to the table. They sip it while waiting for their meal to be cooked and served.

The tea leaves used for bancha, a lower-grade tea, are from the three-year growth (leaves and twigs) of a variety of tea bushes. Bancha is customarily dry roasted before being used for teas.

To make it, dry roast the green leaves in a heavy skillet for 2-3 minutes on medium heat. Stir continuously to prevent scorching. Cool and store the browned bancha in airtight tea caddies.

Add 1 tbsp. roasted bancha to 3 cups boiling water. Lower the heat and simmer the bancha for approximately 15 minutes. Serves 4-6.

To steep: Put bancha leaves in a ceramic teapot. Add boiling water and steep for several minutes. Strain the bancha and serve hot in *yunomi* (ceramic mugs without handles).

SHO-BAN (SOY TEA)

This is a combination of soy sauce (sho-yu) and bancha. In Japan, soy tea is considered a pick-me-up, to be made if a person's energy is waning slightly during any time of the day.

Add 1-2 tsp. soy sauce to your daily cup of bancha. Serves 1.

GENMAI CHA (BROWN-RICE-BANCHA TEA OR POPCORN TEA)

Genmai cha is probably the most popular tea among the Japanese. It is drunk several times a day and it may be served at mealtimes. Genmai cha is now imported to the West. In exporting this tea, some of the rice pops into little white pieces that resemble popcorn; thus genmai cha is sometimes referred to as "popcorn tea."

Dry roast unpolished brown rice in a heavy skillet over medium heat for approximately 10-15 minutes or until the rice is a deep brown color. Stir continuously to prevent the rice from scorching. Combine with an equal amount of bancha leaves. Put in a pot of boiling water (2 tbsp. of the mixture per 2-3 cups of water) and steep for 10 minutes. Strain and serve. Sweeten if desired (it is usually drunk sweet). Serves 4-6.

HOJI CHA (ROASTED TEA)

A poorer grade of bancha, this tea is roasted to enhance its flavor, giving it a smokey taste. *Hoji cha* is imported in tea-bag form and in loose leaves to the West. It may be served hot or cold.

KUKI CHA (STEM TEA)

Kuki cha is a poorer-grade tea made from the larger leaves and the stems of the tea plants. It may be served at mealtimes.

KO CHA

Ko cha is a powdery, less-expensive commercial tea that can be purchased at most marketplaces. It can be drunk instead of bancha in the afternoon or during informal occasions. The water used for *ko cha* must be hotter than that used for higher-grade teas in order to extract the essences.

SENCHA (INFUSED TEA)

This is a common commercial tea in Japan. Unlike bancha, sencha is younger tea leaves, not containing any stems. It is picked during the month of

May. Sencha is often served to guests, or to "special customers" by businesspeople. There is even a Sencha Tea Ceremony, with several schools for learning it.

Warm a *kyushu* (a porcelain teapot) with boiling water. Pour out water. Put 2 tsp. sencha leaves into the teapot. Add 1 cup boiling water that has been removed from heat for a few seconds to lower the heat to about 120 degrees F.

Steep the tea for 1 minute. Pour a small amount into each cup. Add more hot water to the teapot and steep again for a minute. Repeat this process. Sencha cups are never filled to the top. Sencha is served in teacups that are wider at the brim, narrower at the bottom, and generally smaller than normal Japanese teacups. They can hold about three and one-half mouthfuls of tea, almost half the amount of other cups. The *kyushu* used for the Sencha Tea Ceremony, smaller than other teapots used by the Japanese, holds about one cup of water. Most Japanese teapots have a wire-mesh strainer built into the teapot in front of the spout.

Traditional Tea Recipes from Around the World   145

About three o'clock in the afternoon, the Japanese often drink sencha and serve sweets to guests and neighbors. The *okashi* (desserts) are usually made of *yokan* (azuki-bean or kidney-bean paste), sugar, and agar. The desserts are flavored with fruits, nuts, or even tea.

GYOKURO

This tea is considered the finest in Japan. Made from the tips of first-flush leaves, it is sweet with a green color, deep flavor, and strong fragrance. Like sencha, the key to making gyokuro is to lower the temperature of the tea water from the boiling point down to about 120 degrees F so that the leaves infuse better.

Put 4 tsp. gyokuro leaves into a warmed teapot. Add ½ cup hot water (not boiling). Steep for about 1½ minutes, no more. Pour small amounts into 4 warmed cups. Then add more hot water to the teapot and steep the leaves again. Repeat this process until the teacups are filled. Each time the leaves are reinfused, a slightly higher temperature of water is needed. Serves 4.

MATCHA/HIKI CHA (PULVERIZED TEA)

Matcha is the tea used in the Japanese Tea Ceremony. It is ground and powdered from tender young gyokuro leaves.

Put 1 tsp. of matcha in a *chawan* (tea bowl). Pour in a small amount of hot water (about ½ cup) and mix the tea and the water into a paste with a bamboo whisk. Then slowly add a bit more water to the paste and beat with the whisk until a frothy tea is made.

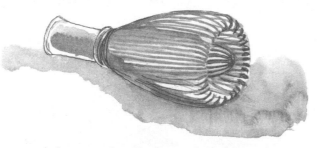

A Japanese bamboo tea whisk (chasen).

KOCHA

When foreigners visit Japan, they can purchase black tea in restaurants. The Japanese prefer black teas imported from India, Sri Lanka, and Indonesia.

The Japanese refer to kocha as American-style tea because it is prepared in the American way. Black tea is served in porcelain cups with saucers. A wedge or twist of lemon may be served on the side. Most often an artificial cream made from a vegetable extract is used to whiten the tea. *Kuriimu* (cream) and *sato* (sugar) are present on the table to be added to the tea, as desired.

KASHMIR

The people of Kashmir make their tea in copper pots, believing that the copper enhances the taste. They prefer a strong brew. In some areas of Kashmir, the samovar is used and the pot of tea essence that sits on top has an exceptionally strong infusion in it. Tea is not drunk with milk here. (For a tea essence recipe, see "Turkey.")

CHAI TULCH (RED POTASH TEA)

Chai Tulch is a rather unusual type of tea made by combining in a pot tea leaves, red potash, aniseeds, and a sprinkling of salt.

KENYA
(FORMERLY BRITISH EAST AFRICA)

In Kenya, tea is grown in highland areas at altitudes of 6,500 to 10,000 feet above sea level. It is cultivated on small holdings and estates in eastern, central, rift-valley, and western parts of the country. Kenyan tea, with its distinctive red or coppery tint, has a delightful brisk taste. Kenya exports this tea to over forty countries around the world.

The people of Kenya drink black tea made from loose leaves. It is usually drunk sweet, the most common sweetener being *sukari,* white sugar manufactured from sugarcane. Generally, two teaspoonfuls of sugar are added to a cup of tea. The majority of tea drinkers in Kenya also add *maziwa,* milk.

Tea is drunk from *kikomvi* (porcelain cups and saucers), *glassi* (glasses), or metal mugs. The amount of tea leaves used varies according to personal preference. Tea in Kenya is prepared by both boiling and steeping methods.

CHAI (BOILING METHOD)

Heat the water in a cooking pan. Add the desired amount of milk. Just before the milk-water starts to boil, add the tea leaves (1 tsp. per 6 oz. liquid) and let the ingredients boil together. Stir the tea with a tablespoon while it is boiling until the preferred color is achieved. Strain the tea into a teapot and serve.

CHAI (STEEPING METHOD)

Heat up water in a pan until it boils and then remove it from the stove. Pour it into the teapot. Add tea leaves and stir the ingredients together. Let the tea stand for about 5 minutes. Strain through a metal sieve into cups. Serve with milk.

CHAI (TEA-BAG STEEPING METHOD)

Boil the water and the milk in separate pans. Place 1 tea bag in a cup (with the desired amount of sugar). Pour the boiling water over the tea bag and steep. Remove the tea bag and add hot milk in desired amounts. Serves 1.

KOREA

TEA UNDER UNIFIED SILLA (668-935)

Tea was introduced to Korea during China's T'ang Dynasty by a Korean named Kim Taeryom who returned from China with tea seeds. The seeds were planted on Mount Chiri, in the south of Korea.

The association between Buddhism and tea drinking may well have begun in Korea rather than in China. While initially tea was drunk for medicinal purposes, it is believed the Korean aristocrats in the T'ang period began drinking it in teahouses while sitting around an image of Buddha. It is also thought that Koreans may have introduced Buddhism and tea to Japan, almost one hundred years before tea was documented as coming from China to Japan.

TEA IN THE KORYO PERIOD (935-1392)

Tea in this period was served at ceremonies such as marriages and funerals. It was made with powdered tea shaved from a tea cake. Tea was also utilized by Korean monks, who drank it to help them stay alert while meditating. The Taoists, who travelled about at this time, may have been responsible for spreading tea drinking in Korea. They also used the beverage to treat colds and as a general tonic.

TEA IN THE YI PERIOD (1392-1910)

Later, during the Korean Yi Period, which corresponds with the Ming and Ch'ing dynasties in China, tea was made from loose green tea leaves steeped in hot water. Tea drinking declined as Confucianism became more prevalent. Wine drinking became more common, except among monks. Heavy taxes were levied on tea, thereby decreasing its cultivation at the monasteries.

TEA IN KOREA TODAY

Today, Koreans import most of their tea from Japan. The tea water is heated in a *chujonja* (kettle). Water heated below boiling point is considered better for infusing green tea leaves. To attain this temperature, Koreans pour the boiling water into their ceramic teacups first. Then they slide the tea leaves down a short section of split bamboo into the kettle. The water from the cups is then poured back into the kettle, where the leaves are allowed to infuse.

Koreans are also fond of sucking raw eggs from the shells between sips of tea. Although tea is drunk throughout the day, traditionally it is not served at mealtimes, as rice wine or spirits are preferred with meals. Both *Lemon Chá* (tea with lemon) and *Naenghong Chá* (iced tea) are made in Korea.

LIBYA

Tea in Libya is almost always made by women. For example, when company comes to visit, the women of the hosting household will retire to a separate room for the sole purpose of preparing the tea for guests. In the room, a gas camping stove, an enamel teapot, a tray, and tea glasses will be brought out from their storage places. The women will sit on cushions on the floor while elaborately preparing the tea.

The method of making tea in Libya is about as unique as one can find anywhere in the world. To a 4-cup-size pot filled with boiling water, 5-8 *tablespoons* of tea leaves and nearly a *pound* (2 cups) of sugar are added. The ingredients are boiled for what seems forever (20-30 minutes).

Libyan tea is served on a silver engraved tray. The tray is laid out with a tea-testing glass, many small pyrex tea glasses, and an equal number of large glasses filled with water. When the tea is thought to be "done," one woman will pour a small amount into the testing glass. She will hold it up to the light to check the color and consistency. If these are not satisfactory, the tea from the glass will be thrown back into the teapot and the tea will be boiled for *even longer.* Once it shines in the light properly, it is poured into the small pyrex glasses. This is done by holding the teapot high above the glasses, tipping it, and allowing the tea to stream down into the glasses, one by one, until they are all filled.

Guests usually drink a glass of tea in one gulp, chased by a large glass of water. It is a mandatory custom in Libya to drink two glasses of tea at every tea sitting. The same tea leaves are used to make the next batch of tea. Water and more sugar are added to the pot and the tea preparation begins all over again.

Favorite accompaniments are *sumak,* canned fish sprinkled with dried red peppers, and *khobza,* a small bun-sized bread similar to a French baguette.

MALAYSIA

In Malaysia, tea (*te'h*) is grown in the state of Selangor and in the exquisitely beautiful Cameron Highlands. It is mainly East Indian Malaysians who live and work on the tea estates. The estates provide housing, medical care, and a good standard of education for the workers and their children.

MALAYSIAN HINDUSTANI CHAI

A modified version of *Hindustani Chai* (see "India") is made in Malaysia. This tea is available in restaurants and cafés, and from street vendors. To make it, place 1 tea bag in a plastic tumbler and fill it three-quarters full with boiling water. Infuse the tea bag until a strong brew is achieved. Then remove the tea bag and stir in lots of sweetened condensed milk. If an even sweeter tea is preferred, add sugar to taste. Serves 1.

TE'H TARIK

Malaysians enjoy an interesting method of making tea that combines their Arabic-African background with their southeast Asian heritage. *Te'h tarik* is usually made by a "tea maker." First tea is brewed in a large pot, then poured into 2 very large metal cups. Sweetened condensed milk, a favorite of southeast Asians, is added.

The tea maker then holds one of the cups up high in one hand and the other cup down low in the other hand. Then, in a tea-making style that originated in Africa, the tea maker will fling the milky tea back and forth between the cups until it is aerated. When bubbly, t'eh tarik is poured into glasses.

MONGOLIA

TARTAR CHAY

Lu Yu in Part III of the *Ch'a Ching* (A.D. 780) described the appearance of tea:

> Tea has a myriad of shapes. If I may speak vulgarly, tea may shrink and crinkle like a Mongol's boots. Or it may look like the dewlap of a wild ox, some sharp, some curling as the eaves of a house. . . . (Francis Ross Carpenter, trans. [Toronto: Little, Brown & Co., 1974])

In the fifth century, the Mongols first encountered tea from China. At that time, the Chinese prepared tea as a medicine, or they added salt and flavorings and served it as a hot, souplike drink. By the twelfth century, the Chinese custom of drinking a souplike tea was giving way to drinking tea without additives. The Mongols continued, however, to add salt, fat, and milk. Because the Mongols consume mainly a meat diet, tea provides some of the vitamins and minerals that they might not obtain due to the absence of fruit and vegetables in their diet. The Tartar souplike pot is believed to be the forerunner of the Russian-style samovar.

To make Tartar Chay, break off tea from a tea brick and mash it into fine pieces. Place a large handful into a kettle of water and heat over charcoal fire until the tea infusion is thick and dark. Salt may be added as the tea is boiling. Milk is then added and the tea-broth is poured into cups.

Another version of Tartar Chay is made by powdering the tea leaves and preparing a strong brew. To the strong tea, a creamy butter and milk mixture is added, followed by the addition of rice. The "tea soup" is brought to a boil, salted, and then served in bowls.

MOROCCO

During the 1850s when British ships were banned from trading in the Baltic by the Russians, the English sailed to new countries looking for buyers of the tea cargo that they were stuck with on board. They managed to dump off a few chests of tea on the Moroccans, thus launching tea drinking in that country.

In time, Morocco became a tea-drinking nation. Today, it is one of the world's largest importers of green tea from China and Taiwan.

In Morocco, a delicacy served with tea is *tmar mahchi* (stuffed dates). There are many ways of making tea here, with as many flavoring ingredients added to it. In fact, there are so many variations on the tea drink that there is a Moroccan adage that claims with pride, "No two cups of tea ever taste the same in Morocco."

Some Moroccans use the Russian-style samovar to heat the tea water. On special occasions, they may make their tea in a silver or brass Manchester-shaped teapot, also known as a Moroccan-style pot. This style of teapot, which originated in England, is elongated rather than round, with a longer spout.

Each guest must drink three cups of tea at a sitting, according to the national custom. During a formal occasion, it is most often the eldest woman of the household or at a gathering who will have the honor of serving the tea.

Moroccans have some spectacular social rituals attached to the making and enjoyment of tea. A tea maker may hold a teapot in each hand high above the cups, dispensing tea from both at the same time. The tea may be served on beautiful silver trays that have been etched in various artistic designs.

In everyday life, however, Moroccans make their teas in different types and sizes of pots and teapots, and drink their teas from a wide variety of cups and glasses. Just as no two cups of tea ever taste the same in Morocco, perhaps for informal tea drinking, no two pieces of tea equipment ever look the same either.

NANA #1 (MINT TEA)

Mint tea is one of the most popular teas in this Mediterranean country.

1 cup hot water
3 tsp. green tea leaves (suggest Gunpowder)
Handful of mint leaves
Sugar to taste
18 oz. boiling water

As your guests are watching, put a small amount of hot water in the teapot. Swirl it around and then throw the water out. This warms the teapot. Now add the tea leaves and a little more hot water, allowing for the wet tea leaves to adhere to the teapot. Next, a handful of fresh mint leaves and sugar to taste are added. In Morocco, sugar is always added to the pot and not to the cups. Pour in 18 oz. boiling water and steep the ingredients for a few minutes. Serve in small glasses or demitasses. Serves 6.

Variation: Use 1 tsp. green tea leaves, 5 small mint leaves, 1 tbsp. sugar, and 6 oz. boiling water. Serves 2.

NANA #2 (SPEARMINT TEA)

Prepare mint tea using spearmint, the most commonly used of all the mints. This is a very sweet and refreshing tea. Don't forget to do the fancy pouring described above.

BERDAAN-NANA MAH SHAY AKHDHAR (ORANGE-BLOSSOM-MINT GREEN TEA)

Place 1 tsp. of orange blossoms, a few mint sprigs, and Gunpowder tea leaves in the teapot. Steep the ingredients together. Add sugar to the teapot to taste.

SHAY AKHDHAR WA ZHOURAT (GREEN AND SAGE TEA)

During the winter months when mint leaves are in short supply, Moroccans may add a few leaves of sage or marjoram to their green tea. To make sage tea, use the mint tea recipe, substituting sage leaves for the mint leaves.

MYANMAR (FORMERLY BURMA)

LEPPET-SO (PICKLED TEA)

Leppet-so is made from decomposed tea leaves. To decompose the tea, fresh tea leaves are kneaded for about 10 minutes to extract their natural juices. The damp leaves are then stored in a cement pit that has been lined with bamboo. The tea is pressed down, covered by planks, and allowed to decay for 2-3 weeks or more. After the fermentation period, the wet tea leaves are removed from the pit. They turn dark immediately upon exposure to the air.

To make *Leppet-so,* the fermented tea leaves are washed in salt water. Oil and garlic are added. Dried fish or other seafood may be added to this tea meal too, depending on their availability. This unique method of fermenting and preparing tea is common among the Shan tribal peoples of Myanmar, Thailand, and southern China.

Because of the geographic contours of the land, many of the people of Myanmar are mountaineers. *Leppet-so* plays a very important part in their everyday diet. When journeying throughout the mountainous areas, travellers take their salty tea meal, stored in the hollows of bamboo shoots. They may consume *Leppet-so* up to thirty times a day for sustenance.

NEPAL

Tea is always served sweet in Nepal. In fact, it is considered rude to serve tea without sugar. The quantity of sugar added by the server communicates the degree of affection or respect for the guest. Thus, a very sweet tea served to a guest can mean

"I like you a lot; you are a very special guest," or "I honor and respect you." When a young woman serves a very sweet tea to an admirer, this could well mean she has a crush on him. On the other hand, if there is a noticeable absence of sugar in the tea served to a suitor, hopefully he will get the hint and not return to bother the young woman again.

CHIYA

Tea in Nepal is made by adding ½ glass of hot black tea made in the usual way to ½ glass boiling milk. Lots of sugar is then stirred into the milky tea.

Note: Milk *(dudh)* in Nepal is not pasteurized, so it must be boiled for awhile.

For a special tea: Add 1-2 tsp. powdered instant coffee to milky tea. Instant coffee is used in Nepal by those who can afford the import for a special occasion.

THE NETHERLANDS

In 1657, Holland's Dr. Brontekoë (nicknamed "Mr. Good Tea") publicly hailed the miraculous benefits of tea. He prescribed drinking 40-50 cups of tea a day to reduce high fever, and if that were not enough, he thought drinking 100 cups of tea a day would be okay.

SCHOTEL DRINKEN (SAUCER DRINKING)

In the 1600s, the more refined Dutch women observed proper tea-drinking etiquette by drinking their tea from saucers, as was a custom of the time. This practice is still in use in some of the rural areas of Holland.

Pour tea from the teapot onto a saucer. Sip (slurp, really) from the rim of the saucer. The saucer should rest on the tips of your fingers, as on a tripod. This method of drinking tea should occupy your time almost exclusively as your beautiful shallow porcelain saucer has to be refilled and refilled, perhaps a dozen times.

SAFFRAAN TAY (SAFFRON TEA)

An early recipe, from the 1600s.

Add saffron threads to boiling water in a pot. Cover and steep for 5-10 minutes. In another teapot, make green tea. Mix desired amounts of saffron-flavored water and green tea in saucers. Add sugar to taste.

ANYS-STER THEE (STAR-ANISE TEA)

Around 1674, the Dutch imported star anise from China, as well as green tea. Dutch women would add a few star anise to the pot when steeping their tea leaves. The Chinese were also experimenting with anise as a flavoring for tea at this time. It is quite likely the Dutch adopted this custom from them.

TEA IN THE NETHERLANDS TODAY

As in the days of their Indonesian colonization, the Dutch still import their tea from the islands in the Malay archipelago (formerly the Dutch East Indies). Breakfast fare for the Dutch is tea and the traditional smorgasbord-type snack of open-faced sandwiches. Slices of bread are served smothered in butter and topped with cheese and thinly sliced meats such as liver, blood sausage, and ham. Children are given a sweet milky tea for breakfast. Adults usually prefer a straight infusion.

In Holland, a large pot of tea (10 cups) is made for a family. To make it, 2 heaping tsp. of tea leaves are placed in the pot, hot water is poured over, and the tea is steeped for 5 minutes. The Dutch are known for reusing their tea leaves. They are left in the pot and more water is added to them after the first round of tea is served. The first tea is served light, while following cups may be more bitter tasting due to the lengthened infusion time. Tea is served in small cups, about 4 oz., which is somewhere between France's 3-oz. demitasses and England's 5-6-oz. teacups.

Lunchtime in Holland brings open-faced sandwiches again, similar to the breakfast fare. Occasionally whole sandwiches are prepared ahead of time to accompany the tea.

While midmorning usually brings a coffee break in Holland, 3:30 in the afternoon is reserved for the *thee-tyd,* the tea break. Favorite accompaniments to fit the Dutch sugarholic taste buds are: *biscuitjes* (biscuits), *chocolatjes* (pieces of chocolate), *koekjes* (shortbread cookies), *muisjes* (candied chips with aniseed flavoring), and *petit fours* (small frosted cakes).

Tea is also served just after dinner. Adults relax in the evenings with sugared tea and perhaps some chocolate pieces.

For more formal tea drinking, fine china teacups and saucers are used and, of course, many people possess the Netherlands' famous delftware. Quilted teapot covers are also popular. The family of my editor, Nina, sets the teapot in a basket with a quilted inlay and then places a quilted tea cozy over the pot, allowing it to be covered from top to bottom. These cozies and inlays are available in matched sets and are used in the Netherlands today.

Contemporary-designed, large-quilted cozies, constructed like large ladies' purses, are the latest cozy vogue. The "tea purse" is set on the table. After tea is poured, the pot is set within it and the sides of the purse are clipped together. The tea purse sits closed in the center of the table until the next sips of tea are desired.

NEW ZEALAND

New Zealanders are the second largest consumers of tea per capita in the world. They prepare it the same way the British do. No doubt the British colonization of Australia and New Zealand influenced the tea-drinking customs of these nations. The countries of the Commonwealth of Nations are the largest consumers of tea in the world.

MAORI TEA

The Maoris, the aboriginal people of New Zealand, drink copious amounts of tea in a day. They use a brick tea, chipping off large pieces of it. The tea chunks are placed in a huge pot filled with boiling water over a campfire.

Some Maoris, especially the women, experience bloating in the abdominal area. The abdominal bloating is referred to as a "tea belly."

NORWAY

To sweeten tea, a Norwegian will often place one or two sugar lumps *(sukker)* in his/her mouth. The sugar dissolves as the tea is sipped slowly.

Scandinavians are largely coffee drinkers. However, there is an afternoon teatime at which time snacks such as open-faced fish sandwiches may be served.

To request tea in Norway, ask for:

Te uten fløte: tea without cream.
Te med fløte: tea with cream.
Te med sition: tea with lemon.
Te med sukker: tea with sugar lumps.

POLAND

HERBATA

Although Poles are mainly coffee drinkers, they also enjoy drinking black tea, which they refer to as *herbata*. In Poland, imported teas are available in grocery stores and delicatessens. Black tea grown in Georgia (formerly of the Soviet Union) is the most commonly imported tea.

There are special *kawiarnias,* restaurantlike establishments where Poles go for pastries, liquors, coffee, and black teas. In a *kawiarnia,* Poles are served a tray containing sugar, hot water, cups, and a variety of teas and tea flavorings.

ESENCJA (STRONG TEA ESSENCE)

This is the mainstream method of making herbata in Poland. A strong tea essence (esencja) *is made in a small, one-cup-size* czajniszek *(teapot).*

Two tsp. of loose tea are placed in the *czajniszek*. Boiling water is poured into the pot and the tea leaves are allowed to steep for 10 minutes. Each drink is made by pouring a small amount of *esencja* into a glass. The rest of the glass is then filled up with boiling water. Drinkers can choose the strength of their tea.

HERBATA OR HERBATA PO TURECKU (TURKISH TEA)

Polish people drink their herbata strong. It is often made in a szklanka (tea glass) or szklanka filizanka (teacup). A glass is hot to hold and so it is placed in a Russian-style ikimudh, a filigreed metal holder with a handle. A tea glass can also be set onto a spodek, a small glass plate made specially for this purpose.

In a cup, place ½ tbsp. of loose tea leaves and some *cuckier buraczany,* sugar made from the white sugar beet, a national crop of Poland. Pour boiling water over and steep for a few minutes. When the sugar is dissolved and the tea leaves settle to the bottom of the cup, the herbata is ready to be sipped.

HERBATA CZAJ (DERELICTS' TEA)

Derelicts' Tea is a very strong tea made with a large concentration of loose tea leaves. It is a Polish substitute for "getting high." The "high," of course, is caused by the high concentration of caffeine. Overdosing on the stimulating effects of tea has traditionally been engaged in by derelicts and prisoners in jail. "High" tea has also been used by Poland's teens in the past. It is losing "appeal" now due to the influx into the country of illegal drugs such as marijuana.

2-3 tbsp. tea leaves
1 cup boiling water

Add tea leaves to water. Use a saucer to cover the cup while the tea is steeping.

HERBATA Z CYTRYNA (TEA WITH LEMON)

If lemons are available, hot tea is drunk with freshly squeezed lemon juice. Iced lemon tea (same name) is also enjoyed throughout the year in Poland. Here is the iced version.

1-4 tea bags
8 cups hot water
Sugar to taste
1 lemon

Put tea bag(s) in a large pitcher. Fill with water and add sugar. Remove tea bag(s) when the desired strength is achieved. (The Poles prepare this as a lighter-colored and weaker tea than what they usually drink.) Refrigerate tea. When the tea cools, squeeze in lemon juice. Serves 8.

HERBATA Z MIODEM (TEA WITH HONEY)

This very enjoyable method of drinking tea is done by first spooning honey into one's mouth and savoring the sweet taste. Then, while the taste of honey is still on the tongue, a sip of black tea is taken to wash the honey down.

HERBATA Z MLEKIEM/BAWARKA (TEA WITH MILK)

New mothers in Poland are often given containers of milk by their parents and grandparents. The underlying belief is that if a mother drinks a surplus of milk while she is breast-feeding, her lactating ability will increase. A new mother will continue to add lots of milk to her tea during the months she is breast-feeding.

MALINOWY (RASPBERRY SYRUP)

The Poles make sweet fruit syrups to add to their tea. The most common is raspberry syrup (see "Tea Syrups" chapter for recipe). To suit your own preference for sweetness and raspberry flavor, add desired amount of homemade raspberry syrup to tea.

PORTUGAL

Portugal is a coffee-drinking country. However, tea is available for those who prefer it. Hot water is added to tea bags or loose tea in a pot and the tea is steeped, uncovered, for 5 minutes. It is served with white sugar. A Russian-style tea is also made in Portugal (see "Tea Brewing Methods—Tea Essence").

On the *ristorante* menus in Portugal, the common listing for tea is as follows:

Chá: black tea.

Chá com 2 chársas: tea served in a larger teapot with two cups ("tea for two people").

Chá com leite: tea with milk, which is available for tourists; the Portuguese do not usually add milk.

SCOTLAND

In 1680, tea was introduced to the Scottish aristocracy by the Duchess of York, Mary, who had experienced her first sips of it during a visit to the Netherlands. Within twenty-five years, tea became the daily drink of the ale-drinking Scots. However, in Scotland as on the Continent, tea had its strong opponents. In 1744, some towns and parishes sought to rid Scotland of it because they believed it might cause serious ailments and, "at the very least," cut into the country's income already based on the tax on ale. Well-known Scotsman and jurist Duncan Forbes, an adversary of tea, suggested that a house-to-house search be done at teatime to catch the "criminal" tea drinkers. Punishment for the offense of owning and drinking the tea, he suggested in a written protest to Parliament, should be nothing less than imprisonment. Today, tea is drunk in Scotland the same way as in England. The Scots have developed their own teatime fare, varying from their English counterparts. Accompaniments to tea include Scottish oatcakes, shortbreads, or the Scottish version of drop scones (pancakes).

TEA AND SCOTCH

The word whisky *comes from the Gaelic* uisge beatha, *meaning "water of life." There are two types of Scotch whisky: one made from the malt of barley, producing a heavy, full flavor, and the other from grains, lighter and less flavorful. Scotch whisky comes in a variety of special grain and malt blends—there are over two thousand variations in Scotland alone. Here, whisky must be aged for three years before it can earn the name.*

Add a jigger of Scotch whisky to ¾ cup of tea. This one can burn your throat. To subdue your tea, add milk.

SRI LANKA (FORMERLY CEYLON)

About one-third of the world's tea comes from Sri Lanka. It is the third major tea-producing country in the world, with more than four hundred ninety thousand acres under cultivation. Sri Lanka is also the second largest exporter of tea in the world. Collectively, teas from Sri Lanka are known as "Ceylons."

Tea pickers in Sri Lanka.

In accordance with their colonial heritage, Sri Lankans drink tea much as the British do. It is drunk at breakfast and at an afternoon teatime, but is not served at other mealtimes.

In the heat of a Sri Lankan day, plantation workers drink hot tea to cool off (tea is considered to have a cooling effect on the body). Surprisingly, unlike in some Asian countries, iced coffees and teas are not common here. Tea is drunk straight or with pasteurized, powdered, or condensed milk *(kiri)*.

Sri Lankans also like to drink their tea with about 2 tsp. of sugar per cup. White granulated sugar is used because they believe other types of sugar change the desired taste of tea. Sri Lankans have a habit of vigorously stirring the sugar placed in the porcelain teacups *(coopay gal)*.

Ancient wisdom in Sri Lanka has it that before one makes an important decision, a cup of tea should be quietly drunk to calm the nerves and clear the mind.

There are five golden rules for making tea in Sri Lanka:

1. Use high-quality tea that has been stored in airtight containers.
2. Use freshly drawn water, brought to a fierce boil.
3. Rinse the teapot with hot water to keep it warm.
4. Bring the teapot to the kettle, and not the kettle to the teapot.
5. Allow the tea to brew for 4-5 minutes. Stir the tea in the pot before pouring.

INGURU THAI (GINGER TEA)

Make tea in the usual way with black Ceylon tea leaves in a 4-cup teapot, adding 3 thin slices of freshly peeled gingerroot when steeping the tea leaves. Strain the ginger-flavored tea into teacups. Serves 4.

ENSAAL THAI (CARDAMOM TEA)

In the 1700s, Ceylon was referred to as the "Spice Island" because it supplied the world with cinnamon and other spices.

2 cardamom pods
3-in. piece cinnamon stick, broken into little pieces
4 cloves
½ tbsp. grated orange peel, dried
4 tsp. Ceylon tea leaves
3 cups boiling water

Remove the seeds from the cardamom pods. Take the back of a spoon and crush the seeds to help release their vapors when steeped. Place all the ingredients in a teapot and steep the mixture for 5 minutes. Strain into cups. Serves 4.

Variation: Mix the dry ingredients together. Place 1-1½ tsp. of the mixture into bottom of each cup. Pour boiling water over the mixture and steep the tea for 5 minutes.

SWEDEN

Swedes drink their tea much the same as other Scandinavians. Tea is infused in a pot or teapot for a few minutes. Rock sugar cut up into small pieces may be used as a sweetener. A small piece is placed under the tongue and is slowly dissolved in the mouth as the tea is sipped.

SYRIA AND LEBANON

Tea customs are generally the same in Syria and Lebanon. Tea is imported to these regions from India and Sri Lanka. These Middle Easterners prefer a strong brew, due to the hot weather conditions. Spicy teas are more commonly drunk in Syria's larger cities, like Damascus.

Tea is made in a *brik,* teapot, and served in small, delicate, 3-oz. serving glasses. For more formal servings, glasses decorated with gold filigree may be used. Tea is drunk in the morning and along with the light evening meal.

Guests are always offered tea or coffee, and many businesses serve tea to their most frequent or long-term customers. A small gas stove is kept on the business premises as is an aluminum kettle for heating water. A *brik* is never far away.

SHY BIL YANSOON #1 (TEA WITH ANISEEDS)

1 tsp. black tea leaves
1 tsp. powdered aniseed
6 oz. boiling water
Sugar to taste

Place tea leaves and aniseed powder in a teapot. Pour water over and steep. Sweeten with sugar, if preferred. Serve in demitasses. Serves 2.

SHY BIL YANSOON #2

1 tsp. aniseeds
2 cups boiling water
2 cups hot black tea

Place the aniseeds in a pot of boiling water. Turn down the heat. Let the liquid steep for 10 minutes. Strain and mix the anise liquid with the hot black tea. Pour into demitasses. Serves 8.
Variation: Mix crushed aniseeds with tea leaves in a teapot when steeping.

SHY BIL KURFAI
(TEA WITH CINNAMON)

¼ tsp. cinnamon
1 tsp. tea leaves
6 oz. boiling water

Put cinnamon and tea leaves in a pot. Pour in water and steep. Serves 1.
Variation: Place a 3-in. piece of cinnamon stick in a tea glass before filling with hot tea.

SHY BIL KUROONFULL
(CLOVES IN TEA)

Place a few cloves into the teapot when steeping the tea leaves.

SHY BIL KUSHRAT EL BERTUKAAN
(ORANGE PEEL IN TEA)

Add strips of orange peel (pith removed) to the tea leaves in a teapot. Add boiling water and steep. The orange peel will give the tea a nice fragrance.

TAIWAN (FORMERLY FORMOSA)

Tea is grown mainly in the northern and central areas of Taiwan. It was brought there by Chinese pioneers from Fukien province.

Oolong tea, the most well known of Taiwanese teas, is made up of leaves that are 40-60 percent fermented before they are heat-dried and fired. In Taiwan, green and Oolong teas are common beverages drunk throughout the day. Tea is not served at breakfast, however; a rice or grain beverage is preferred. Snacks do not usually accompany tea drinking, but if some "nibbling" is desired, a bowl of dried melon seeds may be served.

Country people make tea by pouring boiling water over loose tea leaves in a teapot and steeping. It is drunk from small bowl-shaped teacups.

There are two kinds of *cha-yi-zuan* (teahouses) in Taiwan. The most casual is similar to an outdoor French café. Black tea is available, served in glasses or cups, and may be drunk straight or with milk or sugar. The second type is the traditionally decorated Chinese-style establishment. These teahouses are divided into many rooms so customers can be served in privacy. Small ceramic teapots and cups are served on round trays to customers. Hot water is always kept ready for another round of tea.

Originally, there was no tea break in Taiwan; however, the Western-influenced work break is beginning to make itself known in the culture of Taiwan.

FORMOSA OOLONG CHA

1 tsp. Oolong tea leaves
6 oz. boiling water

Place tea leaves in a teapot. Pour water over. Wait until the leaves settle, then serve the tea. Serves 2. As a rule, Oolongs can sustain several infusions.

SHIANG ZI CHA (SOUR-SCENTED TEA)

Sour-Scented Tea is the result of an innovation in storing tea leaves. Tea leaves are stuffed into scooped-out oranges. The oranges are then dried in the sun, sealed, smoked, and dried in a furnace.

Cut the tea-stuffed orange open, scoop the tea leaves out, and boil them in water along with salt or confectioners' sugar. Drink hot or cold.

SHIANG PIAN CHA (JASMINE TEA)

Scented teas became popular in Formosa during the Sung Dynasty. It was once thought that flower-scented teas were created to cover up the smell and taste of low-grade tea leaves. It is more likely, however, that they became popular because of their wonderful fragrances.

Jasmine grows abundantly in southern China and in Taiwan. Taiwan mixes Oolong leaves and jasmine petals and smokes them together, allowing the jasmine fragrance to enter the tea leaves. To make jasmine tea, place 1 tsp. jasmine tea leaves per 6 oz. water in a teapot. Pour in boiling water and infuse the tea for 5 minutes. Serve in Chinese teacups. Serves 2.

LI ZHI SHIANG CHA (LICHEE-SCENTED TEA)

This is an Oolong tea scented with lichee blossoms. It is made the same way as jasmine tea (see above).

TANZANIA

Tea is grown in Tanzania in the northern and southern highlands. It is one of Tanzania's six main cash crops.

Black tea brewed from loose leaves is drunk here. Tanzanian tea has a brisk taste so it is well suited to being mixed with sugar and milk. *Sukari,* granulated or brown sugar, is usually added. *Maziwa,* pasteurized, powdered, or sweetened condensed milk, is added according to personal taste. Tanzanians may choose to drink a hot or warm tea. The milk is boiled and served separately so drinkers can adjust their tea's temperature at any time. Porcelain cups and saucers, metal mugs, porcelain mugs, or even handleless cups are used. Tea-drinking vessels in Tanzania normally hold between 4 and 6 oz.

CHAI YA RANGI
(BLACK TEA—WITHOUT MILK)

Heat water in a pot according to the quantity required. When the water is nearly to the boiling point, add the tea leaves (1 tsp. per 6 oz. water). Once the tea boils, remove it from the heat and serve. If everyone is taking sugar, add the sugar to the pot before serving.

CHAI YA NDIMU (TEA WITH LEMON JUICE)

Add desired amount of lemon juice to the tea, just before sipping.

CHAI YA TANGAWIZI (TEA WITH GINGER)

Add fresh ginger to boiling water in a pot. Once a ginger-flavored liquid is made, turn down the heat and add the tea leaves. Steep for a few minutes. Serve with sugar.

CHAI YA MAZIWA NA ILIKI
(SPICED MILK TEA)

Spiced Milk Tea is drunk mainly in the coastal areas of Tanzania.

1 tsp. cardamom seeds
1 tsp. cinnamon
2½ cups water
2 cups milk
4 tsp. tea leaves
Sugar to taste

Add the cardamom and cinnamon to water in a pot and heat. Add the milk to the liquid just before it begins to boil. Then add the tea leaves and bring the mixture to a boil. Strain the tea into a teapot or a thermos before serving. Serves 4.

THAILAND

Tea is grown in the northern region of Thailand near Chiang Mai. It is also imported from China and Sri Lanka. The Thai sometimes chew salted tea leaves, a custom not as popular now as it was during the earlier days of tea in Thailand. The practice may have originated with the legend of Bodhidharma, a devout Buddhist, chewing tea leaves to help him stay awake during meditation. The habit now seems most common among the tribal peoples of northern Thailand and neighboring Myanmar.

CHA

Green tea is more popular in Thailand than black. It is made by placing tea leaves or a tea bag in a glass, then pouring boiling spring water over and steeping. Tea is drunk straight or with milk and/or sugar. The water used for drinking or making tea in Thailand is bottled spring water, as purified tap water is not available.

CHA YEN (ICED TEA)

Fill glasses with cracked ice. Drip sweetened condensed milk into each glass to one-quarter full, or use milk and sugar. Then, fill glasses to three-quarters full with strong hot green tea. This tea is sweet and milky.

Note: Thailand does not have a dairy industry. Milk products are imported from Denmark.

TIBET

The Tibetan nomads were introduced to tea during the T'ang Dynasty (618-906). These nomads were primarily meat eaters. As vegetables and fruits were missing from their diet, tea may have provided them with some of the nutrients they needed.

TSAMBA (BARLEY MEAL-YAK BUTTER TEA)

This is a drink of the Tibetans although they have introduced it to the peoples of Nepal. The long-haired, horned yaks of the Himalayan foothills and Tibet have been domesticated. These animals provide the peoples of these areas with yak butter, one of the important ingredients for their tea.

Pieces are chipped from a brick of tea and boiled for a long period of time. It is common practice for Tibetans to leave their kettle of tea hanging over the fire coals while they go about their daily chores. Their tea essence is ready and heated for them whenever they want to make *tsamba*. To this extrastrong brew, salt is added. The salt-tea mixture is then churned with butter made from rancid yak's milk.

It is served in wooden or brass cups. Unless the brass cups have been newly crafted, chances are they will be quite tarnished from much use. The tarnished taste is considered part of the tea-drinking experience.

Another method of making *tsamba* is to add a mixture of butter, flour, and parched barley meal to a cup that is half-filled with a strong boiled tea. The ingredients are mashed together until they become a paste. In its paste form, *tsamba* is ready to be consumed.

Tibetans are known to take in endless cups of yak-butter tea in a day, sometimes as many as thirty. Tea is considered an ingredient of a meal, part of the daily sustenance.

TUNISIA

Tunisians drink both green and black teas. Tea is purchased at grocery stores or at the marketplace in 1 kg. packages, or in smaller 100 gm. packages for those who are less able to afford tea in large quantities. At home, Tunisians usually store it in glass jars.

They mostly drink black tea. It is drunk sweet in Tunisia; *sokar* (white granulated sugar) is the first ingredient added to the teapot. The tea is made in stainless-steel pots that are strong enough to withstand the heat from a gas stove or fire. It is also made over a *kanoon,* an earthenware container in which a charcoal fire is made. Black tea is infused for several minutes or much longer, and is served in small (1 oz.) glasses. The infusion time for green tea is shorter.

The tea leaves are always washed before use—boiling water is poured over the leaves in the pot, the leaves are swished around, and the water is thrown out. Fresh boiling water is then added to the tea leaves.

When making green tea, it is common practice for Tunisians to add a few fresh mint leaves to the tea glasses (2 leaves per glass) just before serving the tea. When mint is out of season, dried mint leaves can be used. In that case, they will be added into the teapot to be infused, instead of into the tea glasses.

Tea is drunk after lunch and dinner. It is served to guests in the afternoon. For a more formal serving, beautiful tea glasses (*kissen*) with gold decorations are placed on *oshene,* glass plates matching in decoration. A host may serve tea with two ceramic teapots, one with black tea and the other with green. Pine nuts can be added to the bottom of each tea glass, with a small spoon provided for eating them.

Tea is served with *biscuitjes* (biscuits) or *petit fours* (rich frosted cakes), which no doubt reflects the strong French influence in Tunisia, as it was a protectorate of France until 1956.

To give tea a fragrance, a teaspoon of geranium water is added just before serving. This is a distillation made from the purple leaves of geraniums. It is also used in Tunisia for adding fragrance to pastries.

When ordering tea in a restaurant, only a couple of choices appear on the menu:

Tei ahmar: black tea, served in a small cup or glass.

Tei akhdhar: green tea.

TURKEY

Tea spread to Turkey from China during the T'ang Dynasty (618-906). Even with the strong impact coffee later had in this area of the world, Turkey still remained primarily a tea-drinking nation. Tea cultivation began in Turkey after 1939, mainly for domestic use.

Black tea is made here the same way as in Russia and Iran. The tea plants growing in all three of these countries produce thinner-bodied teas, so it is not surprising that a strong essence is used to make tea. Water for tea is heated in a samovar (see "Commonwealth of Independent States"). A tea essence is made in a teapot and left to brew on top of the heated samovar. Another method is to make an essence in one pot and heat the water for the tea in another pot, thereby using two pots to make tea.

Tea is traditionally drunk sweet. Sugar cubes are added to it in the tea glasses. Some of the elderly people in Turkey still sweeten their tea by placing a sugar cube between the teeth and sipping the hot tea through the cube. Tea is served at almost every meal. Milk is seldom added.

Merchants in Turkey serve tea in their shops to favorite or repeat customers as a business courtesy. Merchants also buy or receive free tea from the local *cayhane,* tea shop, owners. If a merchant is not equipped to serve tea on his premises, he will give his customers tokens to take down to the tea shop. There, customers will be served their tea and will likely purchase delicious pastries such as baklava (flaky honey and nut pastry), *ay coregi* (walnut cookies), *lokum* (Turkish delight), halva (a sweet made from grain, oil, and sugar), or one of the other cherished accompaniments to tea.

CAJ (TURKISH TEA)

1 tbsp. black tea leaves
Boiling water
Sugar cubes (optional)

Turkish samovar.

Put the tea leaves in the teapot. Pour 1 cup boiling water over the leaves and steep them for 10 minutes. If you want to simulate your own samovar, follow the instructions under "Iran." Otherwise, fill a tea glass to half-full with this tea essence. Then, fill the rest of the glass with boiling water. Add sugar cubes to glass, if desired. Serves 1. This recipe may be doubled or tripled.

UGANDA

Tea is the national drink of Uganda. It also is a major export, next to cotton and coffee in economic importance. Tea is grown in the Jinga area of Uganda (near Kampala), the Central Plateau, western Uganda, and on the northern shore of Lake Victoria. These are mountainous areas, where tea can be grown at high elevations.

Tea-drinking customs in Uganda reflect British, East Indian, and Arab influences. Uganda was a British proctectorate until 1962, so many wealthier Ugandans still drink black tea the way the British do. Milk and sugar are added to tea by preference and tea is sipped from porcelain cups and saucers. In the urban areas, pasteurized milk is available. Dairy products in Uganda are obtained from subsistence farming.

Ugandans of East Indian heritage make tea in the Indian tradition (for recipe see Hindustani Chai under "India"). Hindustani tea is milky and sweet.

Poorer Ugandans make their tea by pouring boiling water over loose black tea leaves in a cup, mug, or glass. Lots of *sukari* (sugar) is added. This practice of drinking a very sweet tea shows an Arabic influence, most likely brought to Uganda by Africans from eastern Kenya and Tanzania.

Tea is made with the use of a *banika,* a large enamel-coated kettle. Water may be boiled in the kettle and added to tea leaves in a cup, or the tea leaves may be added and infused in the *banika.* The *banika* is heated on a kerosene stove. Tea is served in *kikomvi,* enamel-coated metal mugs. Snacks of *mihogo* (boiled cassavas), peanuts, or chunks of wheat bread may accompany the drink.

Loose tea can be purchased in Uganda at *dukama,* small, open-air, market boutiques covered with corrugated metal roofs. At the *dukama,* Ugandans also pick up essential goods such as kerosene, potatoes, salt, and beans. Imported teas from the Assam region of India and from Sri Lanka are available, as are tea blends imported from well-known companies such as Lipton and Twining.

Around 1660, tea was introduced to the Dutch colonists at New Amsterdam (New York). Within a decade, the American colonists had become large consumers of tea. However, after the Boston Tea Party of 1773, American housewives carried out a boycott of tea for a full eight months. As a result, the colonists shifted towards coffee drinking, subsequently making the United States the coffee-drinking nation it is today.

Now tea may be drunk during the morning or afternoon "coffee break." In fact, roughly half of the American population drinks tea on any given day. The coffee or tea break is fifteen to twenty minutes long in the midmorning and midafternoon. It is scheduled into the workday to allow American workers to pause and rest from their occupations.

Tea may be drunk straight (black), light (with milk), or sweet and light (with sugar and milk). Many Americans, particularly those of British heritage, start off their morning with an Orange Pekoe grade tea, imported from India or Sri Lanka. Oolong teas are imported from Taiwan and green and scented teas are imported from China.

In keeping with a fast-paced and convenience-oriented society, many Americans have gone the way of "nuked" water. Tea water is heated in a mug in the microwave, after which a tea bag is added and tea is steeped in the usual way. It take 2-2½ minutes to heat the water. The advantage to nuked tea is that, if you are serving a group of friends, it is possible to offer a variety of teas at the same time.

Tea is also made by plugging in an electric kettle and heating water to the boiling point, or boiling water in a teakettle on the stove. The boiling water is poured over tea bags in a teapot and the tea is steeped for 3-5 minutes, depending on the strength desired. It is served in porcelain teacups or in mugs. The mug was an American invention, originally allowing two or more ounces of liquid to be added to one serving.

When shopping at a grocery store in America, one may find shelf after shelf displaying different brands and blends of teas.

NEW YORK SPRING-WATER TEA

In the early English-style tea gardens in their city, New Yorkers liked their tea made with spring waters. Tea gardens were often built near or surrounding a natural spring. However, it is rumored that the actual quality of the spring water wasn't really that good, so tea-garden owners would have on hand a better-quality water imported from another location. Clearly, the springs themselves were the attraction and the idea of spring water in the tea was enough to sell itself. These days, unless you are living or camping near a natural cold spring bubbling out of the ground, you will have to purchase bottled spring water.

Make black tea in the usual way, using fresh or bottled spring water instead of tap water.

CRANBERRY TEA

Place a dozen cranberries in the bottom of a cup. Mash with the tines of a fork. Add tea bag and boiling water and infuse. Tea may be filtered through a cup strainer into another cup. Sweeten with honey if desired. Serves 1.

Variation: Float a slice of peeled apple on top of the tea.

LEMONADE TEA

Juice of 2 lemons, strained (4-6 tbsp.)
1½ cups boiling water
Sugar to taste (suggest 4 tsp.)
2 tsp. tea leaves
Thin lemon slices

Stir the lemon juice, water, and sugar together until sugar is dissolved. Place tea leaves in a teapot. Pour hot lemonade over the leaves and steep for 5 minutes. Strain into cups. Serve with thin lemon slices. Serves 2.

TEA SODA

3-4 ice cubes
2 tbsp. cream
½ cup tea, cooled
½ cup carbonated cola drink or soda water

Drop ice cubes into a tall glass. Pour cream over the ice, then pour in the tea to about the halfway mark. Fill glass with cola or soda water. Stir the tea soda with a long stir stick. Serve this tea with a straw and a long-handled spoon. Serves 1.

TEA-ICE CREAM SODA

1 tea bag
½ cup boiling water
Vanilla or strawberry ice cream
1 chilled bottle ginger ale

Make a strong tea essence by infusing the tea bag in the water for 5 minutes. Place scoops of ice cream in the bottom of 2 tall soda glasses. Pour the strong tea essence over the ice cream in each glass. Fill the glasses with ginger ale. Serve with straws and long-handled spoons. Serves 2.

MOON TEA

American Classic Tea is the only tea grown in America. It is produced by Charleston Tea Plantation on Wadmalaw Island, South Carolina. The company uses no insecticides in the cultivation. They have graciously provided this recipe and the next one so that readers may enjoy this American-grown product (call 1-800-443-5987 to order this tea).

7 bags American Classic Tea
1 gal. fresh cold water
Sugar to taste

Place tea bags in a 1-gallon container filled with fresh cold water. Cap loosely, and let stand at room temperature for 6 hours or overnight. Remove tea bags. Sweeten to taste. Pour over ice or refrigerate.

Note: By using cold water, much of the caffeine remains in the leaves, not in your cup. Caffeine content is thereby reduced by 50 percent.

CHARLESTON TEA PLANTATION
WEDDING PUNCH

4 cups American Classic Tea, brewed then chilled
4 cups apple juice, chilled
2 cups unsweetened pineapple juice, chilled
2 bottles club soda
Fresh orange and lemon slices
Fresh mint

Combine the tea, apple juice, and pineapple juice and refrigerate until ready to serve. Add the club soda, fruit slices, and mint immediately before serving. Serve iced from a large punch bowl. Serves 10-12.

VIETNAM

Vietnam is a coffee-drinking nation; however, green tea is widely consumed here. Both green and black tea are produced. In this hot country, tea is drunk for the cooling effect it has on the body. Blossom and herbal teas are drunk for enjoyment and as medicinals. A myriad of flower-scented teas are available.

Trà dá (iced tea) may be purchased in plastic bags from vendors at street markets. The vendor fills the bag with cold green or flower-scented tea. A plastic band is tightened around the upper lip of the bag, leaving only a small space for a straw to be inserted.

Tea in Vietnam is purchased in *nhung tiêm bàn trà* (tea shops). The teas are stored on shelves in large glass jars. A tea lover will usually buy small amounts of a variety of teas.

Teahouses are very popular in Vietnam. Typical of the south Asian style, they are furnished with large tables and numerous chairs to accommodate big groups. A variety of teas are offered, so each person receives his own porcelain *binh trà* (4-cup teapot) and *chun trà* (handleless teacup). It is not unusual to see a large gathering of people with as many teapots at the table as there are drinkers. If customers are sharing a tea, a large, 12-cup porcelain teapot may be used.

The cups vary in size. Little ones are utilized mainly for the finest of teas, for oneself or for serving guests at home. Small, 1-cup teapots are also available for making small amounts of fine tea.

Tea may also be drunk from *mây ly trà,* which are Western-style teacups or glasses.

In Vietnam, tea is made by steeping. The amount of tea is measured by hand—a large pinch of tea is thrown into the teapot before boiling water is added. In urban areas, the water is heated on gas stoves. In rural areas, a hearth with wood fuel may be used. The following are just a few of the wide variety of teas enjoyed in Vietnam.

TRA BONG (FLOWER TEA)

Whole flowers and flower parts, usually the petals, are used to make teas in Vietnam. Dried flower petals are used for blossom teas in their own right, and are also blended with green tea leaves. As in China, the most popular use for blossoms is in the making of flower-scented teas.

As a rule, the Vietnamese consider sun-dried flowers more valuable than machine-dried flowers for their scented teas.

Vietnamese binh trà *(teapot) and* mây chun trà *(teacups) are often served on a silver tray* (mam bac trà).

THE TEA BOOK

TRA BONG SEN (LOTUS TEA)

Lotus blossoms are mixed with green tea leaves to scent the tea. Once the lotus blossoms are removed, lotus-scented tea may be steeped.

TRA BONG HUONG DUONG (SUNFLOWER TEA)

The sun-dried heads of young sunflowers (before they seed) are added to tea leaves. The heads are removed before the tea is steeped. This is a popular tea in Vietnam.

TRA TUOI (GREEN TEA)

Drop a large pinch of green tea leaves into a 4-cup teapot. Pour boiling water over the leaves and steep them for several minutes. Serve in porcelain handleless teacups. Serves 4-8.

As a rule, the Vietnamese prefer their tea slightly weaker than in other countries. However, some people do prefer a strong brew and will use a large quantity of tea leaves.

TRA CHANH (LEMON TEA)

Squeeze the juice from ¼ lemon into a teapot over tea leaves. After squeezing out the lemon wedge completely, throw it into the teapot as well. Pour boiling water over the tea leaves and the lemon wedge. Steep for several minutes before serving.

TRA DA (ICED TEA)

Iced tea in Vietnam is made by pouring green tea into a tall glass filled with ice.

The Vietnamese have an unusual method of breaking ice cubes. An ice cube is taken in one hand and cracked apart with the edge of a spoon. Cube after cube is broken in this way, until the tea glasses are filled with ice.

TRA GUNG (GINGER TEA)

Ginger tea is taken for its soothing effect on flus, colds, and sore throats.

To green tea leaves in a 4-cup teapot, add 1 tbsp. of peeled and dried ginger. Pour boiling water into the teapot and allow the tea leaves and the ginger to steep for 4-5 minutes. Serves 4-8.

ZAIRE (FORMERLY CONGO FREE STATE, BELGIAN CONGO, DEMOCRATIC REPUBLIC OF CONGO)

Zaire is a major coffee-exporting country. Tea is grown in the eastern mountainous Kivu area. Although it is both a coffee- and tea-drinking nation, tea is favored.

Green tea is drunk at breakfast with small baguettes. People often dunk their baguettes in it.

Green tea using loose leaves is made in *barre-d,* pots of various sizes depending on the group of people being served. It is made by pouring boiling water over leaves in a pot and steeping for a few minutes. The tea is then strained through a small metal sieve into ceramic cups. Sugar is often added, and some drinkers prefer to add a small amount of canned milk as well.

Much More Tea

TEA FOR A CROWD MADE WITH A TEA ESSENCE

8 tbsp. tea leaves
Boiling water

Place tea leaves in a pot. Pour 6 cups of boiling water over the leaves. Cover the pot and steep for 5 minutes. Strain the tea essence into a warmed teapot.

Add a small amount of the essence to a teacup. Fill the remainder of the cup with boiling water. At a large gathering, pass the teapot with the tea essence in it around to guests so that they may add their own desired strength. Serves 20-24.

TEA FOR A CROWD MADE WITH TEA LEAVES

If using loose tea, make a large tea bag by placing 1 cup tea leaves in a large square of cheesecloth (1 foot square) and tying the ends together with a thread or string. Double the space in the bag before tying it to leave room for the tea leaves to expand.

If you are making tea for 44 people, place the bag in a pot containing 2 gallons of boiling water. Turn down the heat and cover the pot. Infuse the tea for 5 minutes. For a gathering of 100 people, double the amount of hot water used. Remove the bag and serve the tea.

TEA FOR A CROWD MADE WITH TEA BAGS

Use 1 tea bag for every 2 people. When making tea for 44 people, drop 22 tea bags into a pot containing 2 gallons of boiling water. Lower the heat and cover the pot. Infuse tea for 3-5 minutes. If you prefer to use 1 tea bag for every 6 oz. boiling water, drop 44 tea bags into the pot. It is advisable to read the instructions on the tea-bag package as some companies, such as Tetley, are now making 2-cup tea bags.

You will need to fill the sugar bowl with about 1 cup of sugar when serving tea to this size of a gathering.

ICE-CREAM TEA

4 cups strong cold tea
4 tsp. sugar
1 cup vanilla ice cream
1 cup whipped cream

Strain the cold tea into a pitcher and add sugar. Cover and refrigerate for about 2 hours. When chilled, pour into 4 tall glasses and add a scoop of ice cream to each glass. Top with whipped cream. Do not mix. Sip the tea through a straw. Serves 4.

MAPLE-SYRUP TEA

Add 1 tsp. of maple syrup as a sweetener to a cup of your favorite tea.

GINGER TEA

4 thin slices fresh ginger
1½-2 cups water
2 tsp. black tea leaves

Heat ginger in water in a covered saucepan for 10 minutes. Place the tea leaves in a warmed teapot. Strain the ginger liquid into the teapot. Cover and steep for 3-5 minutes. Strain. Serve with sugar to taste. Serves 2.

This tea may also be made using 1 thin slice fresh ginger, 6 oz. boiling water, and 1 tsp. tea leaves for 1 serving.

Variation #1: Substitute a 1½-inch piece of crystallized ginger for the slices of fresh ginger.

Variation #2: In either of the above recipes, use green tea leaves instead of black.

EXTRACT TEAS

Add a few drops of almond, brandy, peppermint, or strawberry extract to a teacup filled with your favorite tea.

TEA WITH ESSENCE WATER

Essence (orange juice, lemon juice, blackberry juice,
  berry syrup, etc.)
Boiling water
Black tea leaves

Mix a few tablespoons of essence with boiling water to make a flavored water. Pour the boiling essence water over tea leaves in a warmed teapot. Infuse the tea leaves for 3-5 minutes. Strain and serve. Sweeten if desired.

FRUIT TEA

Fruit combinations like strawberry-kiwi or peach-pear are delicious when used to make teas. Make sure fruits are clean, peeled, and seeded before adding pieces of them to the teapot. Vary the amount of fruit to suit your taste. Steep fruit and tea together. Filter tea into cups. Add honey to sweeten, if desired. Another alternative is to serve the tea unfiltered with a spoon so drinkers may eat the fruits from the cup later.

Note: Fruit teas may be drunk hot, cold, strained, or unstrained.

BERRY TEA

Place well-ripened blackberries or raspberries in a small metal sieve. Hold the sieve over a teacup. Press the juice out of berries with a fork until the teacup is one-third full with the berry juice. Fill the rest of the cup with hot tea. Sweeten the tea with sugar, syrup, or honey if desired. Serves 1.

Variation: Spatter tea leaves with blackberry or raspberry juice. Then dry the leaves. Make tea in the usual way, infusing 1 tsp. tea leaves in 6 oz. of hot water for 5 minutes.

ROSE-HIP-PEKOE TEA

1 tbsp. powdered rose hips
1 cup boiling water
1 tea bag of pekoe-grade black tea
Sugar to taste

Stir rose hips into water in a cup. Cover with a saucer and steep for 5 minutes. Just before serving, swish tea bag around in the cup to give the rose-hip liquid a mild tea taste. Sweeten with sugar. Serves 1.

A TEA FOR DAVID

I have created this tea in appreciation of my friend David, who spent an uncountable number of hours at the word processor typing this book through its various drafts. Love and affection, David.

2 egg whites
1 tsp. sugar
½ recipe Lemonade Tea (see index)
2 tbsp. sugar
1 tbsp. concentrated lemon juice

Make a meringue by beating the egg whites with 1 tsp. sugar until the mixture is stiff and forms peaks. Pour hot Lemonade Tea into an oven-proof cup. Pile the tea high with meringue and place the cup in the oven under the broiler. Let the meringue brown lightly (approximately 3 minutes).

While the meringue is browning in the oven, make a small amount of lemon syrup in a saucepan by heating the sugar and lemon juice until the sugar dissolves and the mixture is transparent and smooth. Drizzle the lemon syrup over the browned meringue before serving the tea. Serve tea with a spoon. This tea is particularly decadent, and the more meringue, the better.

Note: The cup may be hot to the hands and lips right after it has been removed from the oven.

Festive Teas

ENGLAND

MULLED TEA

Tie dried fruits and spices in a 5-inch square of cheesecloth with a thread. Leave enough room at the top of the bag for the dried fruits and spices to expand. Examples of mulling fruits and spices that can be used are:

Dried fruits: apricots, apples, currants, peaches, raisins, etc.
Powdered spices: allspice, cinnamon, cloves, mace, nutmeg.
Whole spices: aniseed, cardamom pods, cloves, cinnamon sticks, fennel, star anise.
Citrus peels: orange, lemon, lime.
Ginger: thin slices of peeled gingerroot.

Steep tea and the mulling-spice bag in a teapot filled with boiling water. Remove the mulling bag and serve the tea. Sweeten with sugar if desired. Lemon or orange juice may be added to the mulled tea for a citrus taste.

Note: A mulling-spice bag may also be dangled in wine, juice, or a mixture of liquids to spice the beverages.

THE NETHERLANDS

SLEMP

Slemp is served to children at birthday parties or gatherings. It is a hit at Sinterklaas parties during the Yuletide season.

2 cinnamon sticks
6 whole cloves
½ tsp. aniseeds
½ tbsp. orange peel
½ tbsp. lemon peel
4 cups whole milk
1 tea bag (suggest Darjeeling)
2 tbsp. cornstarch
2 tbsp. cold water
6 tbsp. fine berry or brown sugar

Make a mulling bag by tying the spices and citrus peels into a cheesecloth square. Add spice bag to the milk in a pot. Warm the milk slowly and bring it to a light boil. Then turn down the heat, cover, and simmer the milk and spice bag for 45 minutes. Remove scum from milk. Add a tea bag to the mixture for 5 minutes. Remove the tea bag and the mulling bag. With a fork, mix the cornstarch and water in a bowl into a smooth paste; add with sugar to the slemp. Stir continuously for 10 minutes until the slemp thickens. Serve in mugs. Serves 4.

Note: When using citrus peels, make sure the white pith and the white pith threads have been scraped from the inside of the peel. The white pith produces a bitter taste.

Anijsmelk (Anise Milk): Use 1 tbsp. of aniseeds in the cheesecloth. Omit other spices and citrus peels. In Holland, *anijsmelk* is served during or after a skating outing on the canals. Pieces of chocolate often accompany this drink. In Holland there is also a powdered anise product that can be added to warm milk to make an instant *anijsmelk*.

Kaneelmelk (Cinnamon Milk): Use 1 extra cinnamon stick in the cheesecloth. Omit other spices and citrus peels.

Saffraanmelk (Saffron Milk): Omit mulling bag and add 5-6 strands of saffron directly to the milk as it is simmering. Allow saffron threads to stay in slemp for 15-20 minutes and then remove them with a filtering spoon or a small cup strainer. If powdered slemp is used, add 3 pinches of saffron powder to either spicy slemp mixture or slemp with other spices and citrus peels removed.

RUSSIA

HANUKKAH TCHAI

This celebratory way of serving tea for Hanukkah among Russian Jewish people is much like *Café Royale* in France. A sugar cube is soaked in brandy or vodka, and then placed on a teaspoon filled with warmed brandy or vodka. The teaspoon is then balanced across the mouth of a cup of tea. The alcohol is lit and the flaming cube is dropped into the tea.

UNITED STATES

HOT SPICED CRANBERRY TEA

It wouldn't be Christmas in the United States without the delicious taste of cranberries.

4 cups apple cider
4 cups Cranberry Cocktail
Choice of mulling spices (see Mulled Tea)
A pot of hot tea, with leaves strained out (4 cups)
Brown sugar (optional)

Heat all the ingredients except the tea and sugar to a near boil in a pot. Turn down the heat, cover the pot, and simmer the mixture for 15 minutes or longer. Remove the mulling spices and add the tea. Sweeten the mixture with brown sugar, if desired. Serve hot in punch glasses or mugs. Serves 12. This recipe may be halved or quartered to serve a smaller gathering of friends. The leftover punch also tastes excellent when chilled.

APPLE-CIDER TEA

6 cups apple cider
6 cloves
3 cinnamon sticks (2-in. pieces)
2 tea bags
3 tbsp. brown sugar
Thin lemon slices (optional)

Put cider, cloves, and cinnamon in a medium-sized, stainless-steel pot. Cover and heat on medium. When the mixture is hot and steaming, add the tea bags and infuse until the apple cider takes on a light tea taste (approximately 5 minutes). Remove the tea bags and dissolve the sugar in the mixture. Strain the liquid into glass cups or mugs. A transparent slice of lemon may be floated on the top of each cup. Serves 5-6. A single serving can be made with 1 cup apple cider, 2 cloves, 1 cinnamon stick, 1 tea bag, and 2 tsp. brown sugar. Infuse the tea bag for 3-5 minutes depending on the strength of tea taste you prefer.

TEANOG

Eggnog became popular in the United States in the 1770s. It is essentially a blend of milk, raw eggs, and sugar. Cream may be used instead of milk. Various essences can be added to eggnog for flavoring. The eggnog served at Christmastime usually contains brandy, rum, or wine.

1 tea bag
½ cup hot water
Brown sugar or honey (optional)
2 eggs
1 cup chilled milk
¼ tsp. vanilla

Infuse tea bag in water for 5 minutes. Remove tea bag and sweeten tea essence with brown sugar or honey if desired. Put tea essence and remaining ingredients in a blender. Blend until eggs develop a light, bubbly froth on top of the liquid. Serve in a tall glass, in a teacup, or in a punch glass.

Orange Teanog: To the teanog recipe, add 2 tbsp. or more of frozen orange-juice concentrate. Omit the vanilla.

Note: The teanog recipes may be doubled or tripled. For varied tastes, sprinkle any one of the teanogs with ground aniseeds or ground cardamom.

Tea Ices and Iced Teas

TEA ICE CUBES

Into an ice-cube tray, pour a double-strength tea. Sugar may be added and dissolved into the tea. Freeze, then use when desired. Tea ice cubes may be added to cocktails, iced teas, tea punches, and frappés.

BERRY ICE

Heat 2 cups of freshly squeezed berry juice (squeezed through a cheesecloth from 4 cups berries) and sugar to taste (suggest ½ cup) until the sugar is dissolved. Freeze liquid in ice-cube trays. Use the berry cubes in iced teas and tea punches where a fruit flavor is required.

Variation: This recipe can also be made by using 1 cup berry juice (squeezed from 2 cups berries), 1 cup water, and sugar to taste.

LIQUEUR ICE

Mix your favorite liqueur with a strong tea brew. Freeze the mixture in ice-cube trays. Serve liqueur ice in cocktails and in frappés when crushed ice is called for.

BRANDIED ICE

4 cups hot tea
2-3 jiggers brandy

To a pot of tea, add brandy. Pour this mixture into 2 ice-cube trays. Freeze. Use for iced teas, frappés, and teas where a touch of brandy is preferred. (Also see Brandied Tea at end of chapter.)

Note: 1 jigger = 1½ oz.

TWINING'S METHODS FOR MAKING ICED TEAS

The following methods are taken with permission from Twining's "Capture the Moment with Twining Tea: A Connoisseur's Guide."

There are two basic methods for making Iced Tea:

The hot-water method: Follow the same steps for brewing hot tea except that you add one additional spoon of tea leaves or one additional tea bag to what you normally use for hot tea.

In a pitcher, place a little sugar at the bottom and fill it with ice. Once the hot tea is brewed, strain it over the ice which will melt down, leaving half a pitcher of iced tea; top with cold water and refrigerate.

When serving iced tea, garnish with a slice of lemon or cucumber or with a fresh mint leaf.

The cold-water method: In a two-quart jar, place desired quantity of tea bags or loose tea (depending on how strong you like it, 9 to 12 tea bags or teaspoonsful of loose tea). Fill with freshly drawn cold water; cover tightly.

Keep in a cool place from 6 hours to overnight; mix occasionally. Strain. Made in this way, the iced tea doesn't get cloudy and can be stored in the refrigerator for a couple of days. To serve, pour over ice cubes in a tall glass.

OVERNIGHT ICED TEA

The Stash Tea Company suggests the following recipe for iced tea.

6 tea bags
4 cups fresh cold water
Ice

Place tea bags in a 1-qt. container and add water. Refrigerate 7-8 hours or to taste. Remove the tea bags and serve tea over ice. Serves 4.

MICROWAVE OR STOVE-TOP ICED TEA

Also from The Stash Tea Company.

4 cups fresh cold water
6 tea bags
Ice

Boil 2 cups water in a microwave or on the stove. Add tea bags. Brew 5 minutes or to taste. Add 2 cups cold water. Serve over ice. Serves 4.

CRANBERRY COOLER

Thin orange or lemon slices
1 cup hot tea
1 cup cranberry juice
Sugar syrup (optional; see index)
Ice

Add orange or lemon slices to freshly brewed hot tea. Mix in cranberry juice. Chill. Sweeten with sugar syrup if desired. Pour over ice into tall glasses. Serves 2.

Frosting glasses: When serving coolers, frosting the rims of the glasses provides a decorative touch. Dip the glass rims in lemon juice and then into superfine sugar. Or take a quarter-wedge of lemon and rub a ¼-inch band around the glass rim. Dip the moistened rim in sugar.

ICED LEMON TEA

2-4 tea bags (to taste)
Boiling water
1 cup sugar
Juice from 1-2 lemons

Place tea bags in a 1-qt. pitcher. Fill with boiling water. When the tea is the strength you prefer, remove the tea bags. Sweeten with sugar. Refrigerate for a couple of hours. Just before serving, add freshly squeezed lemon juice. Serves 4.

ICED TEA AND FRUIT

2-3 well-ripened apples or peaches
** (peeled and cored or pitted)**
1 recipe Iced Lemon Tea (above)

Chop fruit into 1-inch pieces. Place in the bottom of your pitcher. Add Iced Lemon Tea over the top of the fruit. Serves 4.

FRUITTI ICED TEA

Fill half of a pitcher with strong iced tea. Fill the other half with your favorite blend of fruit juices.

There are so many combinations of mixed fruit juices on the market today. Any one of these may be experimented with to create your own fruit-flavored iced-tea drink.

Vary the proportions of iced tea to fruit juice to suit your taste.

ADD FRUITS TO ICED TEAS

Add fruits in season to iced tea. Serve iced tea with fruits decorating the rims of the glasses or lay fruits around the saucers when serving ice teas in teacups.

CARIBBEAN ICED TEA

Countries in the Caribbean that were influenced by the British like to drink their tea hot or cold.

Put a couple of bruised mint leaves in the bottom of a tall glass. Fill with cracked ice. Pour in a lightly steeped tea. Serve with lemon wedges. Serves 1.

TROPICAL ICED TEA

Fill a blender half-full with crushed ice. Add 4 tsp. sugar and 1½ cups strong, cold tea. Cover and blend on high speed for 1 minute or until the iced tea is thick and creamy. Pour into tall glasses. Serves 4.

ICED CONSTANT COMMENT

Constant Comment is an orange-spice-flavored black tea developed by Ruth Bigelow, pioneer and co-owner with her husband of R. C. Bigelow Company, a tea company. While trying out her own tea blend on guests at a party, a friend remarked, "I've had nothing but constant comment about your tea." Constant Comment has become the company's biggest selling tea.

Place 2 Constant Comment tea bags in a pitcher. Fill with boiling water. When tea is steeped to the color and taste preferred, remove the tea bags. Add sugar to taste. Refrigerate the tea for a couple of hours.

RUM ICED TEA

Fill a tall glass halfway with cracked ice. Pour 1 oz. of dark rum over the ice. Then fill the glass with your favorite tea blend. Sweeten with sugar. Serves 1.

BRANDIED TEA

For a cool drink, place 2 brandied ice cubes in a teacup (see Brandied Ice at beginning of chapter). Fill the cup three-quarters full with hot tea. Sweeten with sugar or honey if desired. Serves 1.

TEA FRAPPE

Serving frappés instead of a dessert is a nice way to end a dinner party.

Pour cold tea into ice-cube trays and freeze. When frozen, put the tea ice cubes in a blender and shave or crush. Fill frappé or liqueur glasses with the ice. Pour your favorite liqueur(s) over top of the ice.

THE TEA BOOK

Tea Syrups, Milks, and Liqueurs

SUGAR SYRUP

Depending on the sweetness and thickness you prefer, sugar syrup may be made with varying quantities of sugar and water.

2 cups sugar
1 cup water
Or 2 parts sugar to 1 part water

Put the sugar and water in a well-cleaned, nonreactive, stainless-steel saucepan. Heat the mixture on medium heat, dissolving the sugar by stirring frequently. When the syrup is transparent and smooth, it is ready.

Refrigerate the syrup in a clean, seal-tight canning jar. The syrup will store for up to 1 month in the refrigerator. Use it to sweeten cold or iced teas, as granulated sugar does not dissolve easily in cool liquid. Also use sugar syrup as a sweetener when making liqueurs.

BERRY SYRUP (RASPBERRY, BLACKBERRY)

2 cups berries
¼ cup water
1 cup sugar

Put berries in a bowl and mash them well with a potato masher. Strain the juice through a cheesecloth or jelly bag until you have a clear juice.

Place the water and sugar in a saucepan and stir over medium heat until the liquid is smooth and transparent. Add the berry juice and bring to a rolling boil. Remove the syrup from heat and pour it into well-cleaned or sterilized jars with seal-tight lids. Refrigerate. Makes just over 2 cups.

Add berry syrup as a sweetener and flavoring to your favorite hot black tea or iced tea, when desired. The syrup will store in the refrigerator for 3-4 weeks.

LEMON SYRUP

1-2 lemons
1½ cups water
2 cups sugar

Peel off the yellow rind from the lemon(s). Be sure to scrape off the white pith. Bring the lemon peels and the water to a boil in a stainless-steel saucepan.

Turn down heat and simmer for 15-20 minutes. The liquid will reduce to about 1 cup. Strain the liquid into another saucepan. Add the sugar and stir the mixture over medium heat until the sugar syrup becomes smooth and transparent. This recipe may be halved.

Orange Syrup: Substitute freshly squeezed orange juice for lemon peels and use only 1 cup sugar. Add a little lemon juice to the syrup for extra citrus flavoring if desired.

Store the citrus syrups in clean, sterilized bottles with seal-tight lids. Citrus syrups may be stored for up to 1 month in the refrigerator. Add citrus syrups to tea as desired for sweetening and flavoring.

COCONUT MILK

Use this flavored tea milk in tea as you would use plain milk. Serve it in a small pitcher, so guests can pour their own desired amount. To prevent the milk from curdling, always add it to the teacup before the hot tea is poured in.

1 cup sweetened shredded coconut
1 tbsp. sugar
1 cup milk

Place coconut and sugar in a bowl. Pour milk over. Cover and refrigerate overnight. Strain through a metal sieve. Makes approximately 6 oz. Pour desired amount into teacups before adding tea.

FLAVORED MILK

Mix your own flavoring (e.g., molasses, maple syrup) into milk. Serve in a pitcher as you would serve milk with tea.

BLACK-TEA LIQUEUR

Tea liqueurs are made by combining a tea essence, a spirit, and a sweetener such as sugar.

5 tbsp. black tea leaves
1 cup hot water
1 cup alcohol
6 tbsp. sugar

Make a strong pot of tea from the tea leaves (suggest Golden Tippy Assam) and hot water. Strain the tea leaves out after 5 minutes and allow the tea essence to cool. Pour the essence into a sterilized glass canning jar. Add alcohol (suggest vodka) and sugar. Seal the bottle and store it at room temperature for 3 weeks. Makes 2 cups.

GREEN-TEA LIQUEUR

5 tbsp. green tea leaves
½ cup boiling water
1 cup charcoal-filtered vodka
½ cup Sugar Syrup

Make a strong tea infusion with the tea leaves (suggest Gunpowder) and boiling water. Add vodka. Steep for 5 minutes. Strain into a sterilized container.

Add Sugar Syrup (see above) to the tea essence. Bottle the liqueur in clean, dark-colored, seal-tight bottles. This liqueur may be drunk right away or matured for a longer period of time. Makes just over 1½ cups.

JASMINE-TEA LIQUEUR

3 tbsp. jasmine tea leaves
1 cup vodka
½-1 cup Sugar Syrup to taste

Place the tea leaves and the alcohol in a clean jar and seal it tight. Steep the mixture for 6 days. Shake the jar once a day for the first 4 days. Strain the liquid through a cheesecloth into a sterilized, dark-colored, seal-tight bottle. (Filtering can also be done through an unbleached paper coffee filter, set into a funnel.)

Add Sugar Syrup (see above) to the infusion. Seal the bottle tightly and let the liqueur mature in a cool, dark place for 1 month. Makes approximately 1¼ cups.

Tea at the Bar

BASIC AFTER-DINNER TEA RECIPE

To ¾ cup of your favorite tea, add ¾-1 oz. of your favorite liqueur. Milk may be added.

There are many liqueurs that add an exciting flavor to tea—peppermint schnapps and fruit-flavored liqueurs to name a few. Experiment with your tea by adding small amounts of liqueurs at first. Taste test by sipping slowly. Vary the amount of liqueur until you discover your preference.

SWEET ICED TEA AT THE BAR

Fill long-stemmed glasses with crushed ice. Fill each glass to three-quarters full with tea, sweetened with honey. Add ½ oz. or more of your favorite liqueur to each glass. Use cinnamon sticks as stirrers.

CANADA

BLUEBERRY TEA

The aftertaste of this tea reminds some people of the aftertaste of blueberries (hence its name). Grand Marnier is an orange-flavored cordial made by the Lapostalle family since the 1800s. It is a blend of Haitian oranges with fine French cognac. Amaretto di Saronna is a sweet apricot liqueur with a bitter almond flavor. Amaretto is produced worldwide; however, the most popular is the Amaretto di Saronna from the small northwestern Italian town of Saronna, where it originated. The apricot kernel is a close relative of the almond, which is why a strong almond flavor emerges when the kernel is blended with the apricot pulp. A romantic legend has it that a woman created Amaretto for her lover to symbolize her love and affection for him.

199

To a 1-cup mug of hot tea, add ¾ oz. Grand Marnier and ¾ oz. Amaretto di Saronna. Serve with a slice of orange and a maraschino cherry. Serves 1.

TEA AT THE LEGION (A VET'S RECIPE)

Canadian whiskies are among the finest in the world. They are blends made from a barley, corn, and rye distillation, and are matured for at least three years before going to market. Canadian Club whisky, sometimes referred to by Canadians as the "Club," is a blend that has been with us since 1858. It is produced by Hiram Walker Company Inc. of Walkerton, Ontario. It is aged in special oak casks. It received its first royal appointment by Queen Victoria in 1898.

Spike your tea with 2 oz. of Canadian Club rye whisky. Or spike your whisky with a wee bit o' tea. Serves 1.

HOT SHOT

Add a splash of tea to your favorite liqueur to warm the liqueur up. Serves 1.

MAPLE-LIQUEUR TEA

Maple liqueur is a sweet, amber liqueur made from the sap of the maple tree. Maple trees are indigenous to eastern Canada.

Add ¾ oz. maple liqueur to a cup of hot tea. Serves 1.

CARIBBEAN

CARIBBEAN TEA

Jamaica was the first country to produce a pungent dark rum. It is made from the fermented juice of sugarcane, cane syrup, and molasses. Caramel is usually added to produce the dark color. Light rum (white), on the other hand, was a Cuban innovation dating back to the 1800s. Light rums are lower in proof than dark rums, as they are aged for a shorter period of time.

To a cup of tea, add 1 oz. of light rum. Serves 1.

Variation: Add the following spices to a pot of steeping tea: 2 cinnamon sticks, a few cloves, and a sprinkle of nutmeg. Once the tea has infused, add a few ounces of Jamaican dark rum to the pot. Serves 4.

GRAND CURAÇAO TEA

Curaçao is made with wine brandy, cinnamon, cloves, mace, and dried unripened orange peels. Grand Curaçao liqueur comes in a variety of colors—orange, brown, white, and green. It was originally made in Amsterdam using unripened orange peels from Dutch Guyana oranges. Curaçao is an island off the coast of Venezuela that was once part of the Dutch West Indies.

Pour 2 oz. Grand Curaçao liqueur into a tall glass. Fill the rest of the glass with 8 oz. hot tea. Stir. Float a thin slice of orange on top of the drink. Serves 1.

ICED CURAÇAO TEA

Place 1 oz. curaçao in a tall glass. Fill the glass with ice cubes. Then add hot tea to fill up the glass. Serves 1.

ENGLAND

NAVY OR SAILOR'S TEA

Add "a helluva lot" of rum to a good ole cup o' tea. Milk and sugar are optional. This tea is a favorite of sailors when they are out at sea.

MINTY TEA

Crème de menthe is a sweetened mint- or peppermint-flavored spirit. It is white or green in color. The spirit used to make crème de menthe is usually cognac. It is excellent as a digestif *after a meal.*

Pour ½ oz. crème de menthe into a teacup. Fill the teacup with hot tea. Add milk as desired. Serves 1.

HOT BUTTERED RUM TEA

2 cut cloves
1 oz. light rum
Hot tea
Sugar or Sugar Syrup
1 pat butter
Cinnamon stick

Place cloves in a cup. Add rum, then fill the cup to three-quarters full with hot tea. Sweeten the tea with sugar or Sugar Syrup (see index). Float a pat of butter on top of the drink. Serve Hot Buttered Rum Tea with a cinnamon stick as a stirrer. Serves 1.

HOT TEA TODDY

2 oz. warmed brandy
Weak hot tea
Sugar Syrup (optional)

Pour brandy into a mug, then fill the mug with tea. Sweeten the toddy with Sugar Syrup (see index), if desired. Toddies may be served with cinnamon, cloves, and powdered nutmeg. They taste good hot or cold.

FRANCE

THE AU COGNAC (TEA WITH COGNAC)

Cognac is a brandy distilled from grapes that are grown around the town of Cognac in western France.

Add cognac to a cup of your favorite tea. Milk may be added to the drink to subdue the taste. *A votre santé!* Serves 1.

THE AU RHUM (TEA WITH RUM)

1 oz. white rum
1 tsp. Demerara sugar
1 cup hot strong tea
1 lemon slice

Place the rum and sugar in a tall glass. Fill the glass with hot tea. Stir to dissolve the sugar. Serve Thé au rhum with a slice of lemon decorating the rim of the glass. Serves 1.

IRELAND

IRISH BREAKFAST TEA

The Irish prefer a stronger brew of tea than do the British. Irish Breakfast Tea is a rich traditional blend of small-sized tea leaves from the Assam region of India. The blend yields a full-bodied tea. Breakfast tea blends usually contain more caffeine than other blends.

Steep up a cup of punchy Irish Breakfast Tea. Add ¾ of a jigger of Irish whisky. Then sweeten it with Demerara sugar. Serves 1.

IRISH TEA

A few whole cloves
A touch of allspice
A pinch of powdered nutmeg
Irish whisky
2 tsp. honey
Strong hot tea
1 cinnamon stick

Place cloves, allspice, and nutmeg in the bottom of a mug, then pour in a helluva good shot of Irish whisky. Add honey, then fill the mug with hot tea. Stir Irish Tea with a cinnamon stick. Serve it piping hot. Serves 1.

IRISH MIST TEA

Irish Mist is a Scotch-based liqueur derived from an ancient Irish recipe rediscovered in 1948. It is flavored with herbs and honey.

Pour a jigger of Irish Mist liqueur into a cup. Fill the cup with a strong brew of tea. Serves 1.

BLITHERING IDIOT

Bailey's Irish Cream is a rich blend of Irish whisky and fresh cream that is delivered to a Dublin-based production plant.

Add 1 oz. or more of Bailey's Irish Cream to a hot cup of tea. Serves 1.

RUSSIA

TCHAI S KRASNIM VINOM

Russians believe red wine added to tea helps one relax. It is also supposed to relieve indigestion.

Pour 1 oz. of red wine into a tea glass. Fill the glass with hot tea. Serves 1.

SCOTLAND

WHISKY TEA

Scotch whisky differs from American whisky in that Scotch whisky uses more barley than corn. Whiskies vary from country to country depending on the qualities of the grains and on the proportions used by the whisky companies. Distillation methods vary as well.

Mix a hearty shot of Scotch whisky with hot tea. This can be considered a hot tea or a hot whisky, depending on the amount of each. Serves 1.

TEA OF THE GLEN

Glen Mist liqueur is a blend of herbs, spices, honey, and a fine Scotch whisky.

Add ¾ oz. Glen Mist liqueur to a cup o' tea. Serves 1.

UNITED STATES

"WHISTLE DIXIE" TEA

Cointreau is an orange-flavored liqueur that utilizes brandy as the spirit and orange peels as the essence. In 1849, the "House of Cointreau" was established at Angers in France. Southern Comfort is a bourbon-based whisky flavored with peach extract and citrus essence. It has a distinctive, strong, sweet taste. It was first made in 1875, in New Orleans, and known as "Cuff and Buttons" or "White Tie and Tails." It was later dubbed "Southern Comfort" by a St. Louis bartender.

Pour ½ oz. each of Cointreau and Southern Comfort into a teacup. Fill the rest of the teacup with hot tea. Serves 1. If you happen to be ordering this drink at a bar, when you want your next cup of tea try whistling "Dixie" loudly to capture the bartender's attention. If that doesn't work, the next time you visit the bar, leave a better tip.

RASPBERRY TEA

Raspberry liqueur is made with the essence of raspberries, a spirit, and a sweetener.

To a cup of hot tea, add ¾-1 oz. raspberry liqueur.

A Home Tea Bar

A tea bar adds a special finishing touch to a dinner party or can stand alone as the focal point for a get-together. Guests can mix their own specialty brew with very little guidance. When serving a tea bar, entertain and impress your guests with your knowledge of teas from around the world. Prepare the following items:

Teas: tea bags of various good-quality blends, and high-quality loose teas (black, green, Oolong, and scented).

Milks: sweetened condensed milk, milk, coconut milk.

Sweeteners: a selection of Demerara sugar, white granulated sugar, sugar cubes, rock sugar, honey, maple syrup, or molasses.

Spices: cardamom pods, cinnamon sticks, whole cloves, ginger slices or crystallized ginger pieces, mint leaves, star anise, ground aniseed, ground cardamom, ground cinnamon, ground nutmeg.

Fruits: orange and lemon wedges, berries of your choice.

Jams: blackberry, raspberry, rose-hip, strawberry.

Liqueurs: a selection of your favorites set out in decanters.

Syrups: sugar syrups made from the recipes in this book.

Let your guests steep mixes of any of the above ingredients in their tea cups. Tea balls, in-cup filters, or one-cup strainers are useful for the steeping.

A NIGHTCAP

Last, but not least, this tea is the one to take with you to bed at night.

Add 1½ oz. Frangelico to a mixture of ½ cup heated milk and ½ cup hot tea. Sweet dreams!

The Word *Tea* Around the World

Ca	Bangladesh
Caay	India, Pakistan (Urdu)
Caj	Croatia, Serbia, Turkey
Caje	Albania
Ceai	Rumania
Cha	China (Mandarin), Hong Kong, Japan, Korea, Taiwan
Chá	Portuguese-speaking countries: Brazil, Macao, Portugal
Cha'h	China (Cantonese, Guandong Province)
Chai	Afghanistan, Egypt, India, Iran, Iraq, Kashmir, Kenya, Libya, Tanzania, Uganda
Chay	Hungary, Mongolia
Cha-yi	Iran
Ché	North Vietnam
Chiya	Nepal
Dé	Penang in Malaysia, Singapore, Taiwan (Hokkien dialect)
Dtik dtae	Kampuchea (Cambodia)
Herbata	Poland
La-pe yei	Myanmar
Nam cháh	Thailand
Nàm sah	Laos
Shai	Zaire (Swahili)
Shay	Ethiopia, Morocco
Shy/chay	Lebanon, Syria
Tay	Israel (Yiddish)
Tchai	Commonwealth of Independent States
Te	Denmark, Iceland, Norway, Sweden, Wales

Tè	Italy
Té	Spanish-speaking countries: Bolivia, Chile, El Salvador, Mexico, Puerto Rico
Tè wátura	India (Sinhalese)
Té/hierbata	Argentina
Tea	Australia, Canada, Great Britain, Ireland, New Zealand, U.S.A.
Tee	Austria, Finland, Germany
Te'h	Malaysia
Teh	Indonesia
Tei	Tunisia
Thai	Sri Lanka
Thé	Algeria, France
Thee	The Netherlands
Ti	Fiji, Papua New Guinea (Pidgin), Samoa, Tahiti, Tonga
Trà	Vietnam
Tsa	Philippines (Tagalog)
Tsa-ee	Greece
Tsamba	Tibet

The Last Drop
from the Author

I wish to acknowledge that there are many tea-drinking countries in the world from which I have yet to obtain tea recipes. It is my hope that with repeated printings of this book, I will be able to include the unique tea customs and recipes from these countries in a future edition.

To the armchair travellers experimenting with the recipes in this book: if any of you would like to share another cultural version of the tea drink with my readers, I would appreciate it if you would write me care of Pelican Publishing Company.

Until then, I would like to part by sharing with you one of the most famous tea quotes in history. These well-known lines are by the Reverend Sydney Smith as recorded in *Lady Holland's Memoirs*:

Thank God for tea! What would we ever do without tea?
How did I exist? I'm glad I was not born before tea!

Sincerely, Dawn Campbell

Glossary

caffeine: an organic alkaloid. There is three times as much caffeine in a cup of coffee as there is in a cup of tea (see "Tea and Your Health" for the amounts of caffeine in tea and its effects on the human body).

polyphenol: a soluble phenolic substance found in plants that, when mixed with water, produces an acidic reaction. Polyphenols give tea its color, body, and taste strength. However, if tea leaves are infused for too long (over five minutes), the polyphenols emitted into the water will be bitter tasting. It was once thought that tannins gave tea its color and body. It is now known that the substances, part of the essential oils in tea, are polyphenols, which resemble tannins in chemical composition.

theaflavins: yellow compounds formed during the tea-leaf fermentation process. They contribute towards the brightness of color and the briskness of the tea infusion.

theine: the same as caffeine, but often used to describe the caffeine in tea.

theophylline: a crystalline alkaloid derived from tea leaves. It is useful as a diuretic and as a stimulant.

vitamins and minerals in tea: tea leaves contain vitamins A, B, C, D, E, K, and P and the elements manganese, copper, iron, iodine, zinc, and magnesium. Vitamin C is lost during the manufacturing of black tea.

Contemporary Chinese teapots.

Index

T